2010

Don Owen

notes on a filmmaker
and his culture

TORONTO INTERNATIONAL FILM FESTIVAL

in conjunction with

INDIANA UNIVERSITY PRESS
Bloomington and Indianapolis

Don

Owen

notes on a filmmaker
and his culture

Steve Gravestock

Toronto International Film Festival Group
2 Carlton Street, Suite 1600, Toronto, Ontario, Canada M5B 1J3

The Toronto International Film Festival Group is a charitable, cultural and educational organization dedicated to celebrating excellence in film and the moving image.

First edition

Library and Archives Canada Cataloguing in Publication

Gravestock, Steve
    Don Owen: notes on a filmmaker and his culture/Steve Gravestock.

Includes bibliographical references.
ISBN 0-9689132-4-5

    1. Owen, Don – Criticism and interpretation. 2. Motion picture producers and directors – Canada. I. Toronto International Film Festival Group II. Title.

PN 1998.3.O95G73 2005   791.4302'33'092   C2005-905172-8

Special thanks to the National Film Board of Canada for the use of photographs from Don Owen's films.

The Canadian Retrospective is made possible through the generous sponsorship of **AIR CANADA** ⊛

Distributed in Canada by Wilfrid Laurier Press
Website: wlupress.wlu.ca

Distributed outside Canada by Indiana University Press
Website: iupress.indiana.edu

Cover and text design: Linda Gustafson
Front Cover Image: *The Ernie Game*

Printed in Canada

for Beverly and Kerri

Contents

cinema
canada

#8   95¢

Clancy 73

Don Owen

notes on a filmmaker
and his culture

Foreword

Although the movies are now more than one hundred years old, it is an exaggeration to say that Canadian cinema occupies just over half of that history. It's true that films made in Canada span virtually the entire history of the cinema, but in reality their production was so sporadic and negligible as to remain unnoticed. Arguably, Canadian cinema was born with the establishment of the National Film Board of Canada (NFB) in 1939. But even this was a half victory. We would not begin to establish a durable feature film industry until the late sixties.

To be a young, aspiring filmmaker in Canada was to travel a lonely road, and few tried until the fifties. When these select few finally set out to pursue their own path, they found themselves on a dirt road rather than a highway. The pioneering director Sidney Furie made a couple of beat-influenced, disaffected-youth films before moving on to England. A fellow traveller who acted in one of Furie's two Canadian films, Don Owen was a young man who made his way from the subsidiary road to the main thoroughfare by driving through the ditch and across the divider, taking a run-of-the-mill docudrama concept and creating one of the formative works of the nascent English-Canadian cinema.

The cultural and social landscapes of Toronto in the late fifties and early sixties couldn't be more different from today. (Much of Owen's filmography charts this evolution with a kind of compassionate, objective scrutiny.) There were no Canadian film production companies in the city making features; in fact, there was hardly any film production at all. Owen

Don Owen, self-portrait

had to go to the NFB's Montreal headquarters in 1960 to receive his apprenticeship. But he returned to Toronto to make his lyrical, elegiac short films, *Runner* and *Toronto Jazz*. They were warm-ups for his first feature, a film planned as a short but that he stretched, without the Film Board's full knowledge, into a feature.

Nobody Waved Good-bye was an accident, and a very happy one at that. It unknowingly established the parameters and laid the groundwork not only for a Toronto-based film culture but also for English-Canadian cinema in general. Its depiction of a middle-class WASP family and its efforts to deal with their rebellious adolescent son captured the disruptions that were beginning to trouble English-Canadian society as it forged ahead into the turbulent sixties. If the film looks naive and awkward to modern eyes, it nevertheless captures the spirit of the times. Its confused, befuddled protagonist—caught between parents, girlfriend and boss, personal aspirations and societal constraints—was a forerunner of so many other confused, befuddled protagonists who would appear in numerous Canadian films in the years to follow.

Owen is a man with a restless nature; when you meet him you are aware of his pent-up energy. His career, like those of many of his contemporaries—Don Shebib, Peter Pearson, Bill Fruet and Larry Kent among them—promised more than it achieved. This is not to denigrate what he accomplished, for Owen definitely left his mark; no student of Canadian film can ever ignore his contribution. But his example points to a collective failure of our culture to create an infrastructure that would support its best artists.

Largely as a result of this lack of support, Owen's career is one of interruptions and hesitations, full of starts and stops. He left the safety of the Film Board in 1969 after the outcry that followed *The Ernie Game*, one of his most daring and interesting works. Later, at a time when funding was being diverted to tax-shelter dreck, he managed to make a number of independently financed films, but in the face of an ever-shifting industry with conflicting priorities, he could never find the momentum necessary to persist.

Throughout the seventies and eighties, Owen would hone his craft, moving from features to short films, from film to television, from documentary to fiction with an almost iconoclastic adventurousness. Regardless of the format in which he worked, he continually spoke to the frustrations, limitations and possibilities of his culture. The primary themes and concerns that recur throughout his works—the sheer effort and alienation inherent in the artistic process; the failed attempts by adolescents to find their place in the world; the historical politics of an amorphous cultural identity—accurately reflect the tensions and challenges that met Owen at nearly every turn of his career.

Piers Handling
Director and CEO, Toronto International Film Festival Group
August 2005

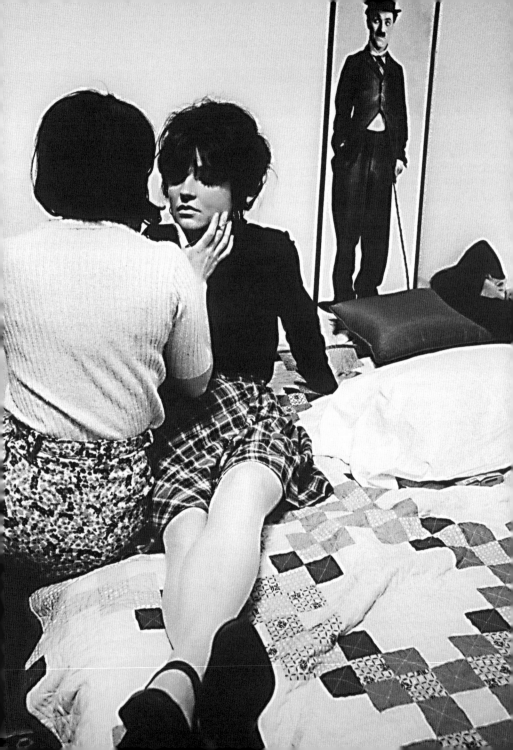

Preface

Don Owen occupies a central place in the development of English-Canadian cinema almost entirely on the basis of his debut feature, *Nobody Waved Good-bye* (1964). Largely considered the first significant feature to emerge from English Canada in decades, *Nobody Waved Good-bye* was a substantial international success, primarily because of the authenticity of its dialogue, much of which was improvised, and its low-key, documentary-style realism. In fact, it was mistakenly perceived as a documentary in some quarters, even receiving the BAFTA (British Academy of Film and Television Arts) award for best documentary feature in 1965.

Owen went on to make several key fiction films and documentaries in the sixties and seventies, most of them for the National Film Board of Canada (NFB), including *Ladies and Gentlemen, Mr. Leonard Cohen* (co-directed with Donald Brittain [1965]); *High Steel* (1965); *Notes for a Film About Donna & Gail* (1966); *The Ernie Game* ([1967], for which he won the Best Director prize at the Canadian Film Awards); and the independently produced *Partners* (1976); *Unfinished Business* (1984), a sequel to his first feature; and his most recent narrative feature, *Turnabout* (1987), also independently produced.

Yet despite his crucial role in the emergence of the English-Canadian feature, Owen remains a problematic and neglected figure. Outside of a few articles, usually focusing on *Nobody Waved Good-bye*, there is little of import written about him. He is not unique in this regard (many of the filmmakers who began in the sixties have been ignored), but Owen probably represents an extreme example. In effect, he's been consigned to the role of pioneer rather than examined as a filmmaker in his own right. And his role as a pioneer is perceived in very limited terms—as if *Nobody Waved Good-bye* was an anomaly, before the real history of Canadian cinema began.

This situation is rather perverse since, on a closer examination, Owen's career is intriguing on a number of levels. Historically, he established many of the key motifs and approaches of English-Canadian cinema in the sixties and beyond. In films like *Nobody Waved Good-bye*, *Notes for a Film About Donna & Gail* and *The Ernie Game*, he was one of the first filmmakers to present Canada as a modern urban country. (Most of *Nobody Waved Good-bye*'s significant cinematic precursors propagated the notion that Canada was a vast, uninhabited nation, rich in natural resources and wildlife, or, as the American literary critic Edmund Wilson put it, "In my youth … we tended to imagine Canada as a kind of vast hunting preserve convenient to the United States.")[1] Owen's presentation of both Toronto and Montreal—the city as a hostile and inhospitable place—was the genesis of a theme that retains currency among Canadian filmmakers.

He was one of the first Anglo filmmakers to explode or mix genres, combining documentary and fiction techniques—an approach that would be reflected in the major works in English-Canadian films in the sixties. Indeed, the mere act of shooting on a Toronto street in the sixties was still virtually revolutionary in the historical context of Canadian cinema. (As Joyce Nelson has pointed out in her book *The Colonized Eye: Rethinking the Grierson Legend*, much of the early NFB product—especially the wartime films—seemed to have been designed to ignore domestic issues entirely.)[2] Owen's early films in particular helped to "de-colonize" Canadian film as an art form, simply by recording life on the streets of Toronto and Montreal. But he was also exploring and documenting Canada's place in the world in geopolitical and cultural terms, most notably in *You Don't Back Down* (1965). Curiously, he remains one of the few English-Canadian filmmakers to directly address our relationship with the United States, an issue reflected in films like *Nobody Waved Good-bye*, *Partners* and, to a lesser extent, *Unfinished Business*.

One reason for the critical oversight of Owen's work may stem from his penchant for trying different means of storytelling, adjusting his approach according to the needs of a specific project. In some ways, neglect of Owen recalls that of figures like the French filmmaker Louis Malle or even John Huston, whose radically varied work ran against the auteurist concept that dominated critical discourse in the fifties, sixties and seventies. (Like Malle, Owen divided his work between fiction and documentary projects.)

Stylistically, little seems to connect Owen's films. From one work to the next, he played with sharply different techniques, searching for the format and style that best suited his material. *Nobody Waved Good-bye* defines and establishes realism as the dominant mode for the English-Canadian feature. The influential Canadian film professor and writer Peter Harcourt sees the film as an extension of the NFB's documentary ethos.[3] However, most of Owen's subsequent work could be called realism only by stretching the definition considerably. The Jean-Luc Godard–influenced *Notes for a Film About Donna & Gail* constantly calls the reality of what's being presented into question through the uncommon device (in cinematic terms) of an unreliable narrator; *The Ernie Game* merges curiously divergent approaches, from highly stylized near-slapstick seduction scenes to scenes that feel like street theatre.

With its gun-toting American industrial spies and its drug-smuggling hero, *Partners* ostensibly belongs to the thriller genre, but it's equally concerned with cultural differences and Canadian history—hardly conventional thriller components. Owen's last film, *Turnabout*, is a cautionary fable about two women who exchange their lifestyles, yet it's also driven by a desire to record life in Toronto's Rosedale electoral riding, a neighbourhood both the extremely wealthy and the very poor call home.

Even among his documentary films, Owen's approach to his material varies considerably. Compare the aloof and elegant *Runner* (1962) with the impressionistic *Toronto Jazz* (1963) or the scruffy, playful *Cowboy and Indian* (1972); the dynamic rapid-fire montage of *Gallery: A View of Time* (1969), a documentary commissioned by the Albright-Knox Art Gallery in Buffalo, N.Y., with the impressionistic approach of *Holstein* (1979), which records the day-to-day life of a dying provincial village. Owen's documentaries are positioned between direct cinema, with its emphasis on highlighting the act of filmmaking and the close identification of the filmmaker with the culture he's recording (practised in Quebec) and the tentative, observational style of the NFB's Unit B *Candid Eye* series.

Yet thematically Owen's work is often surprisingly consistent. His fictional narratives frequently focus on the failings of the old Anglo-Scottish sensibility, which defined and dominated English Canada prior to the sixties and seventies. As Owen puts it, Toronto in the fifties "was like Laura Secord heaven"—an unbearably stuffy place with no real culture.[4] At the same time, Owen is equally suspicious of the cultural and economic influence of the United States, which he sees as potentially invigorating but intensely individualistic and problematic. *Nobody Waved Good-bye*, *Partners* and *Unfinished Business* all concentrate on the drawbacks of both English and American influences. In many ways, Owen adapts and elaborates on themes explored in the forties and fifties by Canadian novelists like Hugh MacLennan, who envisioned Canada, at its best, as a synthesis of American and English values.[5] Owen's account of this conflict is seldom glib, as evidenced by the recurring motif of arrests in his films, which both underlines the significance of rejecting values and strictures and acknowledges a sense of pervasive authority. Whenever someone steps outside cultural norms, the response from authority is immediate.

Similarly, Owen frequently focuses on artists and their place in society, especially in his documentary work, making profiles of such wildly disparate figures as the poet-songwriter Leonard Cohen, the author Mordecai Richler, the avant-garde artist Michael Snow, the painters Robert Markle and Gordon Rayner, the jazz musician Lenny Breau, and the Québécoise chanteuse Monique Leyrac. From the very beginning of his career, he has attempted to define and defend art from a variety of different perspectives. As Edmund Wilson observes, the influence of Protestantism in Canada "notoriously worked ... to discourage the practice of the arts."[6] Suspicion of artists was endemic in Canada. Even in the mid-eighties, the author and critic John Metcalf introduced *The Bumper Book*, a collection of essays on Canadian literature that he edited, by reprinting a recent letter to *The Globe and Mail* in which the writer complained bitterly that all Canadian artists were essentially loafers.[7] (The lack of respect accorded artists and especially earlier Canadian filmmakers is perhaps best reflected in the number of books published on them. The Toronto International Film Festival

Group's Film Reference Library, the premier source for English-Canadian film materials, holds one book each on the directors Don Shebib and Allan King and none on Owen. In contrast, there are nineteen books on John Grierson, the Scot who founded the NFB.)

Owen's interest in this subject seems, in part, to be linked with his inveterate dislike of the oppressive/repressive nature of English-Canadian society, but it also reflects his own ambivalence. Some of his films about artists, in particular the earlier ones, seem determined to defend art in the most Protestant terms imaginable—as viable and difficult work. As his career progresses, Owen moves from this position to defending art as play—as a different kind of necessity, one made even more significant and essential because of the repressive, debilitating culture that opposes it.

As the film historian James Leach implies in "Don Owen's Obliterated Environments," a seminal article on the director's career, Owen's take on this subject shifts markedly between his documentary and fictional work. The artists in the documentaries usually succeed in some fashion, often simply by the act of creation.[8] On the other hand, Owen's fictional films are populated by nascent artists who never act on their talents—for instance, the folkie Peter Mark in *Nobody Waved Good-bye* and *Partners'* would-be photographer, the heiress Heather Grey—or sham artists, like the hero of *The Ernie Game*. Perhaps the lone exception is the television production *Changes* (a k a *Subway or Spain* [1971]) in which the hero rejects a dreary life as a subway-train driver to pursue a career in music. These failed artists—almost invariably presented as isolated, irredeemable figures—are spectacularly "un-Canadian," incapable of observing any proprieties for a significant length of time.

In the same vein, Owen often juxtaposes the playfulness of children or young people with the world of adults, which is typically oppressive, authoritarian or indifferent to the point of hostility. (Canadians seldom seem as young or naive as they do in Owen's films.) That said, Owen doesn't use a simplistic innocence-versus-corruption schema. Characters like Peter Mark and Ernie are nothing if not aggravating and often selfish—and even waiflike and troubled Donna, from *Notes for a Film About Donna & Gail*, is manipulative. Owen refuses to valorize his youthful heroes, instead preferring to criticize the culture they come from. The adults are not normally seen as villains; more often than not they're just as trapped as those they try to oppress.

Much of Owen's work fits into the key paradigms offered by critical surveys of Canadian literature like *The Bush Garden: Essays on the Canadian Imagination* by Northrop Frye and *Survival: A Thematic Guide to Canadian Literature* by Margaret Atwood, both of which outline the lingering effects of colonialism and of course the significance of the natural environment on the Canadian psyche. Owen's artists are prime examples of the urban division of what Frye called the garrison mentality. He argues that English-Canadian poetry reveals an obsession with preserving authority at all costs, which leads to a closed-off protectionist mindset resistant to change. In cities, this resurfaced as fiercely defined cliques and enclaves. Similarly, many of Owen's characters seem cut off, outside the decision-making process or, as Atwood puts it, have "the sense that decisions are made elsewhere."[9] Both Atwood and Frye discuss the existence in works they analyze of unquestioning acceptance of near-omnipresent authority and the prevalent motifs of escape and alienation—both recurring in Owen's work.

At the same time, in films like *Nobody Waved Good-bye* and *The Ernie Game*, Owen makes crucial steps toward realizing that the social order is simply not conducive to the satisfaction of individual needs and ambitions, something Frye defines as a peculiarly Canadian moment of self-realization: "In such a society the terror is not for the common enemy ... The real terror comes when the individual feels himself becoming an individual, pulling away from the group, losing the sense of driving power that the group gives him, aware of a conflict within himself far subtler than the struggle of morality against evil."[10] Owen's characters struggle to identify their real enemies, though they customarily fail. Much of his cinema documents the difficulty of joining the Canadian mainstream—and more often than not this difficulty is a result of poverty and hardship.

Of course, another reason for the critical neglect of Owen's work may be the result of his reputation as a troublemaker, one that extends back to *Nobody Waved Good-bye*, which was originally supposed to be a short docudrama about middle-class juvenile delinquency. Worse, he spoke openly about shooting the film on the sly without the NFB's knowledge, which didn't exactly ingratiate him to the powers that be. (Both *The Ernie Game* and *Partners* proved to be as controversial.)

As we shall see, Owen seemed not to regard filmmaking as a career, and his decisions often flew in the face of professional concerns, most notably his insistence on following *Nobody Waved Good-bye* with a medium-length piece (*Notes for a Film About Donna & Gail*) instead of a feature. Like several of his characters, Owen sometimes seems spectacularly un-Canadian in his willingness to challenge the status quo. (He has been accused of patterning characters in several of his films after himself, most notably in *Nobody Waved Good-bye*, *Notes for a Film About Donna & Gail* and *The Ernie Game*.) Yet another reason Owen was not suitably recognized may be the apparent inconsistency of his work, particularly his later features, though these films are, at the very least, intriguing in the way they advance his characteristic themes.

The form of Owen's career is distressingly emblematic and rather depressingly familiar, reflecting Canadians' habitual suspicion of home-grown work. *Nobody Waved Good-bye* received a nominal Canadian release in 1964. Some of the early reviews were downright hostile—and the industry, or what there was of it at the time, wasn't exactly supportive. (The distributor-turned-producer Nat Taylor referred to it as "amateur night in Hicksville.")[11] Things turned around when the film played the 1964 New York Film Festival and especially after it was picked up for distribution in the United States. The film was subsequently re-released in Canada and received a far more positive response. This situation has been duplicated ad nauseam: filmmakers like David Cronenberg and Atom Egoyan faced significant critical opposition domestically and then achieved success elsewhere before being appreciated at home.

The subsequent neglect of Owen's work is even more disturbing. Paradoxically, *The Ernie Game*, for which he won a Canadian Film Award, effectively halted his career as a feature filmmaker for almost a decade; the tax shelter period of the late seventies—which prioritized genre films over art films—didn't help much either; nor did the lack of critical attention to Owen's work in the intervening years. Referring to the scarce support for emerging writers, Mordecai Richler once joked that Canadians eat their young; it's perhaps equally true that they neglect their elders.

Mon Pays

When Don Owen began his career in the late fifties, almost no film indus-try (feature or otherwise) existed in English Canada. With the exception of commissioned industrial and tourism films and a few sporadically pro-duced features, virtually nothing was going on; certainly there was nowhere for a would-be filmmaker to learn his craft in Toronto, at least outside of television. Private investors were non-existent, and there was no government funding—and wouldn't be until the formation of the Canadian Film Development Corporation (CFDC, now Telefilm Canada) in 1967. From 1954 to 1963, no feature films were nominated for Canadian Film Awards (the precursors to today's Genies), and none were even sub-mitted for consideration from 1958 to 1963. Basically, being an English-Canadian filmmaker was largely unheard of.

In Owen's hometown, Toronto, this situation was exacerbated by the ferociously repressive, buttoned-down nature of the place. "The whole city shut down on Sunday," he recalls. "There was only this kind of WASP com-munity. But in the late fifties the Toronto Film Society had wonderful

Sunday afternoon showings of two films by a director. You couldn't go into a movie on Sunday anywhere else in the city. That's where I came in touch with the auteur idea. I remember seeing [films by] Jean Renoir and just totally freaking out."

Of course, there were a few foolhardy types who tried to make feature films, most notably Julian Roffman and Sidney J. Furie, both of whom partnered with Nat Taylor.[1]

A National Film Board veteran, Roffman made two features with Taylor, both genre films: *The Bloody Brood* (1959) and *The Mask* (1961). *The Bloody Brood* features Peter Falk as a gangster who passes himself off as a bohemian in order to indulge in sadistic games that eventually result in murder. It played off the contemporary interest in beatniks and juvenile delinquency, reflected in American movies like Laslo Benedek's *The Wild One* (1954) and Nicholas Ray's *Rebel without a Cause* (1955). *The Mask* was a very early "head trip" horror movie. It follows a psychiatrist whose patient sends him an ancient, cursed mask that inspires whoever wears it to embark on a killing spree. Neither film was financially successful, though *The Mask*, which was shot in 3-D, did become something of a cult hit.

Both Furie's early Canadian films—*A Dangerous Age* (1957) and *A Cool Sound from Hell* (1958)—were financial failures. But they remain more central in the context of Canadian cinema than Roffman's efforts, largely because they seem closer in temperament to what would follow. A realist piece on many levels, *A Dangerous Age* prefigures what would become the dominant mode of Canadian filmmaking in the sixties and much of the seventies. Which is not to say that the films were entirely devoid of genre trappings; both fit into the same juvenile delinquency sub-genre as *The Bloody Brood*.

A Cool Sound from Hell, now lost, dealt with beatniks and biker gangs; *A Dangerous Age* followed two teenage lovers, David and Nancy, in their attempt to get married against their parents' wishes. (As the Canadian B-movie historian Paul Corupe has suggested, *A Dangerous Age* is not dissimilar to Owen's first feature.)[2] Would-be writer David considers himself a rebel and is prone to rash, pretentious outbursts. (He even lectures the cops on the Magna Carta.) David and Nancy's wedding plans are thwarted

The Mask, Julian Roffman

by their own inexperience. They intend to marry in a small town but soon discover they can't purchase a marriage licence there. Frantic rushing from one town to the next follows, but eventually cooler heads prevail. Nancy returns to her dormitory (after she's arrested for truancy), while David is left alone with a solicitous police officer. The young couple's inability to get married effectively signals the end of their relationship.

Their plans are also undermined by English-Canadian society's innate cautiousness and near-omnipresent authority. As David and Nancy's plans unravel, authority figures pop up everywhere to intercede. Even though their parents are minor presences in the film, the rest of the adult world—including the police and teachers from Nancy's boarding school—intervene to rescue the kids from themselves. Spotting a bridal shop after the first failed marriage attempt, David angrily kicks over a trash can and is confronted by the police, who have instantly appeared on the scene. This aspect of the narrative reflects Margaret Atwood's assertion in *Survival* that "lawful authority ... is seen as the social form of a divine order ...

Canadians are terrified of having authority undermined."[3]

A Dangerous Age portrays a society—characterized by a formidable sense of alienation and by WASP rigidity—that lacks the means to deal with rebellion or any kind of dissent. Even Furie seems to side more with the adults. The kids come across as injudicious and/or dim, while the adults, who are far more attuned to what's going on than David or Nancy would ever suspect, weigh in with cautionary lectures that are never seriously refuted, such as a police officer's remark that David's version of love is "just a case of hot pants."

Intermittently, David's suspicion of the adult world seems somewhat insightful—given the pervasive nature of authority and its smug representatives—but it is frequently undercut. His refusal to leave Nancy alone underscores his fear that she lacks his commitment to their plans and suggests a controlling, bullying nature. Moreover, his firmly held belief that the adult world is inherently phony is challenged by a bit of business with wedding rings: David thinks they'll turn green within a day, but finds his is still in decent shape as the story ends. Also, his rebellion is strangely puritanical, reflecting the repressive nature of his community. At one point, he tells Nancy, "As for nightclubs and stuff like that, those are for people who are bored with each other." One gets the sense that if the film was American, David and Nancy probably would have succeeded in their quest. *A Dangerous Age*, which concludes with the title "Made in Canada," seems less like a fleshed-out drama than a case-study film, which isn't all that surprising, considering that that was probably one of the few kinds of domestic product Furie was really exposed to.[4]

Despite Taylor's assistance, Furie was unable to secure adequate distribution for either *A Cool Sound from Hell* or *A Dangerous Age*, though, in retrospect at least, this doesn't seem to bother Owen very much. "I know what [*A Cool Sound from Hell*] is like. I've seen it, I'm in it. I play a beat poet. I'm so glad it's lost. I'm so relieved [laughs]. It's very much an imitation Hollywood B-movie. They [the films] are okay. [Furie] wanted to go to Hollywood. They were made to get him into Hollywood."

Owen's role as an assistant director on *A Cool Sound from Hell* was one of his first jobs in film. He also worked briefly as a stagehand and writer at the Canadian Broadcasting Corporation (CBC), the only really viable option in English Canada for aspiring filmmakers at the time. He took other jobs where he could find them, one of which proved particularly fortuitous. *Our Man in Muskoka* (1961) was an industrial film with the unlikely premise that Russian agents had been sent to spy on the tourism industry in Canada with the aid of carrier pigeons. On the shoot, Owen met the director, Don Haldane, and the cinematographer, Don Wilder. Haldane, who would go on to make one of the few English-language features at the NFB (*The Drylanders* [1963]) prior to *Nobody Waved Good-bye*, convinced Owen that the best place for him was the NFB's Unit B. Wilder helped pull some strings at the Board's head office, and with that Owen was off to Montreal.

The only true film studio in the country, the NFB had been, virtually since its inception in 1939 under the direction of John Grierson, the official and exclusive source of film production in Canada. However, for many Canadian film historians, including David Clandfield, Joyce Nelson, Peter Morris and George Melnyk, Grierson bears significant responsibility for the dearth of feature film production in Canada.[5] A noted theorist, Grierson was almost slavishly devoted to the documentary form, dismissing fiction film as a "temptation for trivial people."[6] He was equally adverse to long-form filmmaking, which made feature production even more of a pipe dream. Until Pierre Perrault and Michel Brault made the legendary *Pour la suite du monde* in 1963, few feature-length documentary films were produced by the Board. Grierson's emphasis on compilation films in the Board's early years didn't help either.[7]

The other major player in the industry, the federal government, had proven equally ineffectual in its meagre attempts to bolster feature filmmaking in Canada. Although it flirted in the late forties with a proposal to not only institute an import quota on American films but also tax the profits made by American distributors in Canada and funnel this money into Canadian feature film production—a move supported and advocated by Grierson's successor as NFB film commissioner, Ross McLean—this was quashed by the government's weak-kneed acceptance of an alternative proposal tabled by the Motion Picture Export Association of America (MPEAA, now the MPAA). The Canadian Cooperation Project, instituted in 1947, ceded any right by the federal government to impose quotas or levies of any kind in exchange for positive mentions of Canada in American studio films (intended to help tourism) and the distribution of NFB shorts in the United States. The agreement effectively eliminated the possibility of feature film production in Canada and perpetuated the notion—held not only by Hollywood studios but also by Canadian politicians—that Canada is part of the American domestic market for motion picture distribution and exhibition. (In 1922, the American producer/distributor Lewis Selznick famously remarked, "If Canadian stories are worthwhile making into films, companies will be sent into Canada to make them.")[8]

It is largely because of this stifling environment that the importance of the work produced by the Board's Unit B cannot be overestimated in the context of Canadian film history. One of the NFB's key early hires, Tom Daly was the head and spiritual guide of Unit B, the production team at the NFB where most of the best and most innovative work of the fifties was being done, partly because of Daly's devotion to those working there. Some of the essential contributors included the directors Terence Macartney-Filgate, Colin Low, Wolf Koenig and Roman Kroitor, the house writer/narrator Stanley Jackson, the fabled Scottish-born animator Norman McLaren and, later, the legendary iconoclast Arthur Lipsett.

Daly, a skilled editor renowned for his habit of taking elaborate notes on everything he saw, would become Owen's mentor, just as the Unit B ethos would become an important factor in shaping his approach as a director. The Unit B filmmakers inaugurated a radically different aesthetic from that propagated by Grierson in the early years of the NFB. Replacing Grierson's emphasis on compilation films and tendentious voice-over, the directors in Unit B used every technique available to them and often stressed the recording of everyday life in Canada—something Grierson actively discouraged in favour of a more international perspective.[9]

Some of Unit B's major accomplishments include Koenig and Low's *City of Gold* (1957), an account of the Yukon Gold Rush told primarily through still photographs and narrated by the cultural icon/writer Pierre Berton; Macartney-Filgate's *Police* (1958), which explores the job of policing in Toronto and was shot in part by Michel Brault; Koenig and Kroitor's *Lonely Boy* (1962), ostensibly a look at the career of the teenage crooner Paul Anka but also a pioneering account of the meaning and costs of celebrity; Low's *Corral* (1954), a visually striking record of the breaking of a wild horse in the Canadian West, and one of the first NFB productions that didn't use a voice-over; Kroitor and Low's *Universe* (1960), about the birth of the cosmos; and the lovely look at big-city life, *The Days before Christmas* (1958) by Macartney-Filgate, Stanley Jackson and Wolf Koenig.

Unit B was a hotbed of innovation in documentary form and subject matter not only domestically but internationally. The introduction of new, lightweight 16 mm cameras and sound-recording equipment gave rise to advances in documentary practice that occurred simultaneously in the late fifties and early sixties in three countries: France, the United States and Canada.

Coining the term *cinéma-vérité* ("cinema truth") for his influential film *Chronique d'un été* (1961), Jean Rouch, the movement's central figure in France, mixed documentary and fiction and even staged some scenes to create a hybrid form—one that sometimes challenged the documentary form itself (evidenced by *Chronique d'un été*, which culminates in a debate among the subjects and filmmakers on whether the project has succeeded) and was fundamentally different from the Griersonian model, which was alleged to present reality. Rouch's aversion to the assumption that documentaries were objective truth grew out of his experience in Africa making ethnographic films, including *Moi, un noir* (1957). For Rouch, uncertainty was essential for both the filmmaker and the audience, and claims of objectivity were in his view invariably linked to colonialism and imperialism.

In contrast, many of the key filmmakers of the American version, including Robert Drew, Richard Leacock, D. A. Pennebaker and Albert and David Maysles, selected inherently dramatic subjects, ranging from the Cuban Missile Crisis and American elections (*Crisis* [1963] and *Primary* [1960]) to concert tours and/or performances (*Don't Look Back* [1967] and *Gimme Shelter* [1970]). Moreover, "they claimed to be able to record reality, to attain objectivity; they forbade intervention."[10] Usually, the work of these filmmakers is grouped under the rubric cinéma-vérité.

Each country offered different innovations, and Canada was actually responsible for two: the Anglo one propagated by Unit B (often referred to as *Candid Eye* films, after the influential Unit B series of the same name), and the Québécois version exemplified by the early work of Brault, Claude

Jutra (both of whom worked with Rouch) and Pierre Perrault, to name only a few. As Peter Harcourt notes in his essay "The Innocent Eye: An Aspect of the Work of the National Film Board"—probably the first study to identify a distinctively Anglo-Canadian cinema—the English-Canadian version was far more tentative, posing questions but seldom answering them, allowing them to percolate instead; this was a far cry from the propaganda-based aesthetic of the early Grierson years.[11] Many were unscripted, and, as another film historian, D. B. Jones, points out, the aesthetics of the French photographer Henri Cartier-Bresson, particularly his emphasis on capturing the moment, were central to the group's approach.[12]

As David Clandfield says, in the Québécois films (generally categorized as "cinema direct") the filmmakers were perceived to be part of the culture they were portraying and, like Rouch, typically insisted on foregrounding the filmmaking process.[13] The Québécois version, as we shall see, was far more overtly politicized than the English-Canadian. Much of the work from the early sixties by filmmakers like Brault, Perrault, Jutra, Gilles Groulx, Denys Arcand and Gilles Carle focused on distinct aspects of Québécois culture while confronting the stereotypical image of the province as a rural backwater—a dynamic initially evident in Perrault and Brault's seminal work *Pour la suite du monde*.

The Québécois films could—and indeed still can—be read in radically different ways: as ironic, even sarcastic, critiques of contemporary Québécois culture or as celebrations—celebratory simply because the actual culture was being recorded. They could also be very elegiac, as evidenced by Perrault's work. The first significant Québécois foray into this type of filmmaking came with *Les raquetteurs* (1958). Co-directed by Brault and Groulx, this impressionistic record of a snowshoe festival in Sherbrooke, Quebec, seems to admire and mock the goings-on simultaneously. There's a profound sense of community and ritual in the film, which, like *Pour la suite du monde*, culminates in a wild party that reflects the participants' recognition and celebration of their culture's unique nature.

Another factor contributing to the air of celebration, revolution and change percolating in Quebec in the late fifties was the death in 1959 of the long-time Quebec premier Maurice Duplessis and the subsequent end of the *grand noirceur* ("great darkness"), a socially anachronistic and repressive period typified by rampant political corruption and a complete lack of division between Church and state. There were also exciting new film movements springing up internationally, most notably the French New Wave, which, as one might expect, had a significant impact on Québécois filmmakers. Claude Jutra's first feature, *À tout prendre* (1963), was shot on 16 mm outside the auspices of the NFB, and he used many of the techniques for which the New Wave was known, from jump cuts to location shoots. (It also boasts a cameo by the director François Truffaut in a party sequence.)

Don Owen

Owen's eagerness to relocate to Montreal— the production centre in Canadian cinema at the time—went beyond his filmmaking ambitions. Montreal was by far the most interesting and influential city in Canada. Not only had it experienced a lengthy construction boom, but population growth had soared. In 1961, the year Owen arrived, there were 1,750,000 residents— a 60 per cent increase since 1941.[14] Owen's first projects included assignments as a cinematographer on works that proved to be two germinal Québécois films, *La lutte* (a k a *Wrestling* [1961]) and *À Saint-Henri le cinq septembre* (1962). Both films capture aspects of life in what was then Canada's largest city. The list of contributors on the films was a veritable who's who of Canadian filmmaking at the time, including Brault, Jutra, Groulx and the writer Hubert Aquin, as well as Owen's best friend, Arthur Lipsett.

"There was a group of French filmmakers who were very much *séparatistes*, very adventuresome," Owen says, "but Michel Brault had worked for Unit B a lot. He'd shot several of their films and he had learned a lot of those things from their approach, which was candid."

Though Owen was primarily a cameraman on both films, their influence can be seen in many of his own directorial efforts—in the attempts at cultural self-definition in his second short film, *Toronto Jazz*, and even more prominently in features like *Nobody Waved Good-bye* and *Partners*,

which examines the impact of English Canada's British heritage, stretching back to the arrival of the United Empire Loyalists in the eighteenth century. Similarly, Owen would address Anglo-Canadian culture both critically and affectionately. His short seventies documentary *Holstein* (1973), for instance, is a sympathetic portrait of a small town on the wane. *Nobody Waved Good-bye* records the stuffy Anglo nature of sixties Toronto, and *Unfinished Business* captures the city two decades later, invigorated by its increasingly multicultural nature.

Based on "The World of Wrestling," the influential Roland Barthes essay (he's credited as one of the creators of the film) about the ritualistic nature of professional wrestling, *La lutte* examines the phenomenon in Montreal's "wrestling mecca," the Forum. Wrestling was extremely popular in the city during this period, and was one of the most-watched programs on Société Radio-Canada (SRC, the French-language equivalent of the CBC).[15] In his essay, Barthes argues that wrestling has its own specific highly coded rituals; each match enacts a battle between good and

La lutte

over-the-top evil, with a litany of requisite elements emphasizing the suffering on the part of the hero and the punishment of the villains.[16] The emphasis on suffering—typified by the quasi-religious theatrical spectacle of the competitors writhing on the mat in agony—imbues the events with a decidedly Catholic aura, as if medieval morality plays had been updated for modern times. The music, a strangely soothing combination of Bach and Vivaldi, is used contrapuntally, contrasting with the near-abstracted violence of the match, underlining its cheesier aspects and formalized character.

At the same time, the film is more than a mere rendition of the essay. The filmmakers are as interested in the fans' violent reactions and the composition of the audience, which includes everyone from properly attired ladies to grizzled senior citizens in thick sweaters and caps. The crowd responds viscerally to the action. Fights almost break out before the match; there are several afterwards. When one of the tag teams cheats, fans have to be prevented from charging the ring in outrage.

In its own way, *La lutte* was as crucial an act of self-definition as *Les raquetteurs* and in some ways more central. Its sardonic exploration of the Catholic/morality play aspects of wrestling and, perhaps most significantly, its predominantly urban character (combined with the violent nature of the matches) signalled a break with the old images of Quebec as a quaint rural backwater, a dominant theme not only in Québécois films but in Québécois criticism of the period. (Jutra, the province's most prominent and celebrated feature filmmaker of the decade, was ruthlessly pilloried for making rural period pieces like *Mon oncle Antoine* [1971] and *Kamouraska* [1973].)

À Saint-Henri le cinq septembre

Similar in approach but far more lyrical and impressionistic, *À Saint-Henri le cinq septembre* is a portrait of a day in the life of a traditional working-class neighbourhood in Montreal that is dying because of a declining economy. The district (which was also the birthplace of the jazz pianist Oscar Peterson) was immortalized in one of the first major Canadian novels, *The Tin Flute* by Gabrielle Roy, published in 1945 and a success in both French and English Canada. The director's credit for the film was given to Hubert Aquin, the noted political radical perhaps best known for his acclaimed *séparatiste* novel *Prochain episode* (1965).

"It's hard to believe how really forceful it [Quebec separatism] was at that moment," Owen recalls. "I can remember when the RCMP and the army were arriving and people were getting arrested. There was a French guy who had come to Quebec and really got involved in the political movement. And when they didn't arrest him, he went around trying to get arrested. It was considered noble. So he would go to the clubs he thought they were going to raid."

According to Owen, much of the footage he and Lipsett shot for the film wound up being used because, unlike their Québécois compatriots, they were more concerned with following their instincts than investigating the political connotations of what was being recorded.

If anything, *Saint-Henri* is even more sardonic than *La lutte*, tweaking Québécois assumptions about their heritage and the entire filmmaking process as well. The film is driven by an evasive, intentionally contradictory, post-modern voice-over; at times, it interprets events for us, then retracts its claims; at others, it is accompanied by an image that suggests something else altogether. Initially, we're told that the day the film was shot was chosen at random. Later, sounding almost sheepish, the narrator admits that's not exactly true; in fact, it's the first day of school—a day selected because the filmmakers believed it would mean increased activity and afford the opportunity for countless dramas.

À Saint-Henri le cinq septembre

The notion of racial purity is mocked throughout the film. A tour of a pizzeria is accompanied by the narrator's declaration that here you can order "a fine Italian pizza … made by Greeks"; a flirtatious young girl is, according to the voice-over, enjoying herself because she is secure in the knowledge of her French ancestry. Quebec's link to France is further satirized by the narrator's praise of the conveniences offered by North American life—readily available even in a poor neighbourhood like this one but not nearly as prevalent in France, not even in urban centres like Paris. The complacent nature of his claim makes it double-edged; it could just as easily be mocking the North American obsession with creature comforts. The narrator holds forth on the area's racial harmony (many immigrants from African and Caribbean countries settled there), which he says is most evident among children, though we see few shots of children of different ethnicities playing together.

The audience's prejudices and preconceptions are similarly lampooned by the narrator's remark that the stereotype of the miserable, grubby, working-class child is nowhere to be found—perhaps a dig at Roy's novel. The narration and editing also take aim at the pervasive influence of Catholicism. A tracking camera captures houses as the sun descends and comments that all good Catholic families are at home

Runner

listening to religious broadcasts; the filmmakers then promptly chase down the vibrant nightlife. The disparity between dire poverty and sumptuous Church ritual is caustically summarized through a funeral at which a poor resident is given a lavish send-off.

The film is also distinguished throughout by the free-wheeling cinematography, which is especially evident in the opening shots of the neighbourhood as the community wakes up to face the day. This sequence in fact bears a rather striking resemblance to the opening shots of the waterfront in *Chronique d'un été*. (The subjects of the film reportedly despised it, feeling they were being ridiculed.)

Saint-Henri contributed to Owen's work experience not only technically but also in documenting a culture. Visually, the film shares certain motifs with several of his short films. The emphasis on church steeples and departing ships resurfaces in documentaries like *High Steel* (1965) and fiction shorts like *A Further Glimpse of Joey* (1966), while the sleepy, rather hazy opening of *Saint-Henri* is almost replicated in *Toronto Jazz* (1964). The sardonic, contradictory narration, which invariably calls attention to itself, pops up again in both *Notes for a Film About Donna & Gail* and *Turnabout.*

Following *Saint-Henri*, Owen discovered a Toronto-based long-distance runner named Bruce Kidd and decided he would make the ideal subject for his first effort as a director. At the time, Canadian athletics were in a worse state than the film industry—athletes were virtually invisible, internationally speaking, due to inadequate training programs and lack of funding. One of the first Canadian runners to achieve international prominence, Kidd was a staunch nationalist and refused scholarships from American universities. *Runner* follows him as he trains alone in Toronto's Beach district, with other athletes at the North York Track Club and in a race with several international competitors on his home turf.

Runner

Beautifully shot on 35 mm by John Spotton and Guy Borremans, the film emphasizes Kidd's idiosyncratic running style; his arms dangle and flail and his hands seem to scoop at the air. Spindly and smaller than the other runners, he comes across as a David facing an unseen Goliath. With the exception of a brief bit of clowning around at the track club, Kidd is almost always seen alone. In fact, he's effectively separated by the coach's specific attention to him during the training session—it's actually the others who clown around. When Kidd, who was known for his tendency to sprint for the finish line long before other runners, takes off and leaves the rest of the pack behind, the crowd sounds fade and the audience becomes a blur. The forlorn jazz score, modelled on Miles Davis's contemporary work and improvised by the Montreal trumpeter Herbie Spaniard, strengthens this feeling of solitude. (This motif reappears far more prominently in specifically urban films like *Nobody Waved Good-bye, Notes for a Film About Donna & Gail* and *The Ernie Game.*)

As exquisite as the visual scheme is, the soundscape is just as distinctive, most notably in the early scenes in the Beach, combining children yelling, Kidd's own footsteps and a plethora of natural sounds, including a non-existent bee that seems to swoop at the camera; all of it, according to Owen, was created in post-production by Tom Daly.

The commentary, written by the British poet W. H. Auden (who also wrote the commentary track for Grierson's early British production *Night Mail* [1936]) and read by the Toronto actor and musician Don Francks, stresses the amount of work it takes to train muscles to perform at the peak of perfection. In an archetypically Canadian moment, neighbourliness is praised and sore winners mocked, for "sports shall be loved by losers."[17] The commentary inures us to the possibility that Kidd might lose, and we're somewhat confused by his apparent victory. (Indidentally, the decision to use Francks as a narrator was controversial: he didn't sound British enough, a criticism clearly based on the assumption that England was the centre of culture.)

Runner

Runner was a significant success, garnering international praise. The British Film Institute described it as "a poem to the human body which is wholly successful."[18] It also introduces one of Owen's recurring obsessions. Kidd seems to be a kind of proto-artist, cut off from the rest of society because of his unique skills. Owen delivers variations on this isolated artist motif throughout his career, from *Ladies and Gentlemen, Mr. Leonard Cohen* to *The Ernie Game* (where the artist figure is the most ostracized in any of his films).

Despite its sometimes verbose commentary (modelled at Owen's request on Pindar's highly alliterative odes), the film seems akin to Colin Low's *Corral*, particularly in its precise, poetic account of Kidd's training and the act of running itself. Like *Corral*, *Runner* focuses on the activity and the effort that goes into the job at hand.

Intriguingly, the film's subject and dramatic structure—it concludes with a race—virtually begs for a dramatic approach found in the American version of cinéma-vérité, with its emphasis on inherently charged conflicts. (See, for example, the competition for votes in D. A. Pennebaker's

Primary.) But Owen refuses to fully dramatize the events, stressing Kidd's solitude instead. By the last section of the race, Kidd is so far ahead of any of his competitors and for so long a time that his separation/isolation becomes the subject. His eventual triumph is presented in a strangely muted way. The film is easily one of Owen's most lyrical works—and also one of his loneliest.

His next project combined two of his principal obsessions: jazz and his increasing interest in onscreen improvisation. Owen had been fascinated by improvisation since the late fifties, when his efforts to educate himself in filmmaking techniques led to involvement with a group headed by the actor Al Waxman (star of the seventies hit TV series *King of Kensington*), who returned to Toronto in 1959 from working in an Off-Broadway production of *A View from the Bridge* by Arthur Miller.

Toronto Jazz

As Owen explains, "There was a group of young guys that got together, led by Al Waxman, Perry Rosemund [who would produce *King of Kensington* and another series, *The Royal Canadian Air Farce*], Martin Lavut [who directed the feature film *Palais Royale* in 1988], Gordon Pinsent [who would write and star in *The Rowdyman* (1972), as well as direct features and perform in countless films and television shows], myself and two others. Waxman had been to New York; he'd studied with the Neighborhood Playhouse and he'd learned techniques of improvisation. We got together and learned how to improvise—you [would] set up conflicting motivations for the characters, and when they come together there's an explosion. There's like a calculated misunderstanding going on and it's very energizing."

Called *Toronto Jazz*, the film focused on three local bands: the Alf Jones Quartet (with Michael Snow on piano); the Doug Thompson Quintet; and the Lenny Breau Trio (with *Runner* narrator Francks on vocals)—all of them prominent in the city's early sixties jazz scene.

The lineup of talent was substantial. Snow went on to become a prominent avant-garde artist, pushing boundaries in both visual arts and

Toronto Jazz

experimental cinema, as well as founding the Music Gallery, a long-running Toronto institution that showcases groundbreaking music. Breau would become one of the most respected and versatile jazz guitarists in the world, drawing on such disparate sources as classical music and country and western to forge his distinctive style.

The film was intended as a defence of Owen's hometown. He was irked by the Québécois attitude toward Toronto. ("I had already become friends with the Quebec filmmakers," says Owen. "They used to tell a joke that was about a contest in which the first prize was a week in Toronto, and the second prize was two weeks in Toronto.") If *Runner* seemed very much a Unit B film, *Toronto Jazz* was the exact opposite, much closer to the sensibility of *La lutte* and *À Saint-Henri le cinq septembre*. Like the Québécois filmmakers who made those films, Owen was implicated in the subculture he was documenting. He was very much part of the jazz scene in Toronto. It was a creative oasis in the uptight Toronto desert.

The film is structured around interviews with band members and scene-makers like Clem Hambourg, the owner of the House of Hambourg (the prominent jazz club of the time), as well as rehearsals and performances, with copious inserts of the crowd. Francks serves as guide, a slightly nerdy, eager-to-please hep cat, willing to interpret for his colleagues and even prod them when necessary. One of the more memorable sequences has Francks horsing around and improvising a semi-lewd bit with one of Snow's figures from his *Walking Woman* series, when the latter proves to be less than forthcoming for the camera. The effect he creates is something akin to a Beat used-car salesman.

Michael Snow in *Toronto Jazz*

The jazz scene afforded Owen the opportunity to capture improvised moments on film. He and the cinematographer, Borremans, recorded the musicians in performance as well as the reactions of the crowd. (The crowd is almost as present as the fans in *La lutte*, with many inserts of people responding to the music.) The shoot—which followed the philosophy of many Unit B productions, i.e., shooting as much material as possible—wasn't without its challenges, in part because of the enormous amount of material compiled.

The film was Owen's first to concentrate directly on artists and the process of making art, a subject that he would frequently return to. In addition to a portrait of a scene (similar in some ways to *La lutte* and *À Saint-Henri*), the film addresses two issues: why anyone would choose to play jazz in Toronto, and what it means to be a jazz musician. The first question is answered by the drummer Archie Alleyne, who explains that he actually benefits from Toronto being a jazz backwater. He's not influenced by anyone, which keeps his music to some degree pure. Furthermore, since there are so few jazz musicians in Toronto, he's unique.

The second question is far more complicated, and Owen and his collaborators respond with a variety of answers. The act of playing jazz is initially defended in conventional, bohemian Romantic terms: as freedom, addiction, enigma and a battle against the Philistines.

The jazz musician represents freedom, explains Francks, because he refuses to be categorized by his job, unlike the denizens of the straight world who simply put up shingles and define themselves exclusively by occupation. Even the club owners get in on the act. Clem Hambourg rails against Toronto's seemingly endless need to explain itself: "First we were Toronto the Good; now I'm not sure what we are." (In some ways, the city stands in for all of English Canada here, representing what Northrop Frye has identified as its "preoccupation with its own history, its relentless cultural stock-taking and self-inventories.")[19]

The puckish nature of the subjects elaborates on the theme of freedom, contrasting the musicians' willingness to look ludicrous with the stuffy, pristine nature of their surroundings. See, for instance, Francks's massive, ancient Bentley rolling down prim suburban streets; the enormous bassist Stan Zadak dragging his equally enormous instrument across the street; the outlandish dog that Archie and his beehive-coiffed girlfriend take for a walk; Francks carrying a life-size *Walking Woman* down the street; Francks's aforementioned bit with another sculpture, which is alternately lewd, childish and inventive. The jazz scene is also explicitly linked to sexuality: see the countless insert shots of the young women in the audience while the bands perform.

Jazz is defined as an addiction: those who have become hooked on it are incapable of ignoring it. One musician, who moved on to other things at one point in his life, confesses, "Deep down I always had to do it." Art is enigmatic, a mystery, reflected in Snow's reticence when he refuses to respond to Owen's questions about the links between his artwork and his music.

As the band members, and Francks in particular, present it, being a jazz musician is by definition a battle. The jazz scene in Toronto, as Francks says in an early sequence, is exemplary precisely because it's consistently threatened. He and Zadak even describe the process of navigating the scene using battle imagery. At times, Owen's musicians almost perfectly embody Northrop Frye's concept of the garrison mentality. Frye argues that because of the isolated and endangered nature of Canadian communities, citizens develop a "garrison mentality," one that places a high priority on adhering to rules and regulations in order to preserve themselves.

Within cities, the garrisons are simply multiplied.[20] Owen's jazz musicians adhere to their code rigorously, despite outsiders' resentment and lack of understanding.

Perhaps most revealing, however, is the way band members frequently present their work in terms of effort and knowledge, i.e., as viable work— a strangely Protestant rationale for this particular art form. Breau's bassist Zadak explains that you constantly have to push yourself in jazz, since it always changes; he argues that it's physically demanding as well (a familiar refrain if you've ever known anyone who plays stand-up bass). Francks delivers a speech about his band's need to learn the rules of improvisation; in a similar vein, he praises Breau's encyclopedic knowledge of music, noting that Bach serves as one of the sources for a new song. Breau himself was not your conventional jazz musician—his work seems to owe as much, or more, to classical music as to Coltrane or Ellington. It's probably an indication of the film's somewhat divided defence of its subjects that the one song Breau's trio performs live is a blues riff whose refrain states, "I've got papers on you, baby"—a rather WASPy, ownership-based phrase.

Owen's own opinion of *Toronto Jazz* has varied over the years. In the seventies, he told the film journalist Natalie Edwards that he considered the film a failure.[21] It might be more accurate to call it an intriguing experiment. At the very least, the film is a unique record of a rather interesting scene. It was also a seminal film in Owen's own development. Inspired by the experience of *Toronto Jazz*, he would decide to improvise an entire feature.

NOBODY WAVED GOOD-BYE

PRODUCED BY THE NATIONAL FILM BOARD OF CANADA

2

Everybody Knows This Is Nowhere

Originally called *First Offence* and intended as a short docudrama about probation officers and middle-class juvenile delinquency, *Nobody Waved Good-bye* is arguably the first truly significant English-Canadian feature film since the silent-era productions of Ernest and Nell Shipman. It stands alongside Don Shebib's *Goin' Down the Road* (1970) as one of the key fiction films of the decade 1960–70.

Nobody Waved Good-bye was extremely influential for a number of reasons, not least because of the way it was made: the scenes were almost entirely improvised, and its production was apparently handled under the table at the NFB. There are differing accounts of how it came to be. In Owen's version of events, he was heartened by a chance meeting with the NFB commissioner Guy Roberge, who praised the French Unit's determination to seize opportunities rather than waiting for them to be offered. Owen also notes that there were few executives around the summer the film was shot, which allowed him to order stock in a quantity far beyond that assigned to the project and to elaborate on motivations and objectives as the shoot progressed. He has always cited the support of both the executive producer, Tom Daly, and the producer, Roman Kroitor. Conversely, D. B. Jones, for example, claims that Owen's actions were hidden because of an internal power struggle between Tom Daly and the head of production, Grant McLean.[1] The film historian Gary Evans completely dismisses the notion that board executives didn't know what was going on.[2] Regardless, any resistance to the project didn't last long; Owen was allowed to return to Toronto for reshoots.

Nobody Waved Good-bye combines documentary and fiction elements and helps establish what would become the dominant style of Canadian cinema for the rest of the decade. Shot using handheld, lightweight 16 mm cameras, the film garnered much attention and acclaim for its documentary aspects, principally its visuals (indeed, in some circles it was actually mistaken for a documentary), though Owen's improvisational techniques with his cast also contributed to the enthusiastic reception. Similarly, Claude Jutra's remarkable *À tout prendre* mixes fiction and real-life events, which were largely taken from Jutra's own life and restaged. Allan King's celebrated documentaries *Warrendale* (1967) and especially *A Married Couple* (1969) would push this overlap/confusion even further, blurring the line between recording reality and influencing it (via the camera's effect on the participants' behaviour). With the exception of Larry Kent's independently made feature *The Bitter Ash* (1963), *Nobody Waved Good-bye* also represents the first recognizable attempt to record English-Canadian urban realities and middle-class morality in the context of a feature film.[3]

Nobody Waved Good-bye follows Peter Mark (Peter Kastner, then the star of the CBC program *The Time of Your Life*), a middle-class high-school senior from the Toronto suburb of Etobicoke, who is at odds with his parents and their plans for him—indeed, with bourgeois values in general. He states his credo very early in the film: "I can tell you without a minute's hesitation what I don't want to do. I don't want to get in the kind of rut my parents are in … although, you know, on the surface it's fine: a comfortable house, you've broadloom, you have gold fixtures in the bathroom, you go to a good school … Your pants are always pressed. That is what I don't want to do. You know, we've been living in this kind of setup for so long that we've lost all perspective."[4]

Though his final exams are looming, Peter prefers to play hooky with his girlfriend, Julie (Julie Biggs). His rebellious behaviour grows increasingly problematic, and he's eventually arrested while on a joyride in a showroom car that his car-salesman father, Warren (Claude Rae), brings home. (As we shall see, an arrest—often related to car theft—is a recurring motif in Owen's work.) Peter's mother, Mary (Charmion King), kicks him out after he returns home late one night following a hootenanny. He heads downtown to fend for himself and ultimately finds a job in a parking lot. His boss (the late John Vernon, best known as the crusty dean from *Animal House* [1978]), constantly pushes him to short-change the customers. Meanwhile, Peter's parents continue to press him about returning to school. Peter's parole officer finds out about the thefts and is understandably less than pleased; so is his boss, who suddenly decides he wants a bigger cut. (He's angry because Peter, against explicit orders, has been cheating the regulars—or so he claims.)

Nobody Waved Good-bye

Julie's unexpected arrival at Peter's rooming house brings things to a head. She wants to leave town immediately, despite Peter's protests that they don't have enough money. He actually begs her to return home, but she persists, demanding that he ask his father for the money. Predictably, his father refuses, telling Peter he's "a bad investment." Pushed to the wall, Peter steals the float from the parking lot as well as a car, and he and Julie attempt to leave. Julie soon realizes what Peter has done and, after revealing that she's pregnant, insists he turn around or let her out. He chooses the latter option, and drives on alone with tears in his eyes.

Nobody Waved Good-bye seems perched between two sub-genres. It recalls the juvenile delinquency films of the fifties, such as *Rebel without a Cause*, but it's far less melodramatic and more subdued, lacking the fervid Freudian angst of those films. It certainly does not valorize Peter or his suffering the way Nicholas Ray valorizes James Dean's character, Jim Stark. The film is also prescient to some degree, anticipating the spate of mid- to late-sixties films that frequently pandered to the suddenly powerful and immense baby boomer generation. But where Mike Nichols's *The Graduate* (1967), Dennis Hopper's *Easy Rider* (1969) and Mort Ransen's *Christopher's Movie Matinee* (1968)—to use a Canadian example—seem to argue that their protagonists are somehow purer because of their inability to express themselves, *Nobody Waved Good-bye* emphasizes the shortcomings of the parents and especially the society they represent instead of entirely validat-

Nobody Waved Good-bye

ing Peter or his highly atomized (read American), rather inarticulate version of society—though it certainly acknowledges the virtues behind his attempts to rebel. (Owen's film is closer in sensibility to his friend Robin Spry's documentary *Flowers on a One-Way Street* [1967]: an account of a sit-in that took place in Toronto's Yorkville district during the mid-sixties, the film criticizes authority figures far more than it praises protesters.)

While the filmmakers do side primarily with Peter, their presentation of him is decidedly ambivalent. Much of the time, he is not a particularly appealing character.

For one thing, he's a motormouth, always hectoring people sanctimoniously about his beliefs. Following a rancorous dinner dominated by an argument between Peter's parents about his truancy, his sister Jennifer's fiancé, Ron, arrives. Sent to answer the door, Peter promptly attacks Ron for his lifestyle, his presumably placid acceptance of materialist values (he's a dentist) and even his choice of movies (*Cleopatra*, the Elizabeth Taylor extravaganza from 1963).

Similarly, at a job interview in a bank after he leaves home, Peter tells the hiring manager that the position doesn't pay enough to suit him. (He's eventually rejected on account of his attitude.) Rather impudently, Peter asks his parole officer how much he makes, then tells him he mustn't be very good at his job. He blithely informs Julie that car drivers resent people on scooters because they envy their freedom.

At the same time, Peter is not devoid of charm. This is most evident in the scene in which he flirts with a lonely young waitress in a restaurant where he's temporarily employed. Most significantly, Peter is exuberant and energetic enough to ask questions, and tough (or maybe willful) enough to persist when he's unhappy with the responses. Few people, incidentally, bother to give him direct answers.

Peter maintains that he exists in a vacuum and has little or no relationship to any groups, culture or society. In effect, without Julie, he's a garrison of one. All his opinions are criticisms without solutions. (See his credo above.) Most notably, there's the justly famous scene in which Peter confronts Jacques, a young Québécois with whom he's playing chess: "Well, you and all your talk is about identity on a sort of—Quebec, Quebec—we're French Canadians ... I have my own character. I have my own needs. I have my own desires and those are very specific; and I'm not ready to lose myself in a mass of English Canadians so that I can say: *we*."[5] (Peter's opponent is played by Jacques Leduc, a prominent critic and filmmaker.) Jacques tells Peter he's adopting highly individualistic American values,

Nobody Waved Good-bye

which Peter denies. Jacques then pointedly asks Peter what his values are, to which he has no response, and Owen cuts away. (In a significant moment, Peter tries to take a turn before Jacques has moved his piece; the action underscores Peter's characteristic lack of reflection and general pushiness.)

Peter's inability to define what he stands for links him to the anti-heroes of much American fiction of the period, most notably Holden Caulfield in J. D. Salinger's *The Catcher in the Rye* (1951), as well as cultural critiques like Paul Goodman's *Growing Up Absurd* (1960). But it also underscores the juvenile nature of his rebellion, which is purely apolitical and naive—it completely turns on his adolescent need to have his opinions go uncontested.

This is reflected in his relationship with Julie. As Peter Harcourt points out, Julie seems to serve primarily as a sounding board, at least in Peter's eyes: "Julie seems chiefly the mirror in which he can recognize the more attractive aspects of himself."[6] However, she is not without opinions. In one scene, she attempts to debate the issue of self-interest with Peter, but he, as usual, talks over her objections. Her attraction to him hinges on his outspokenness and his rejection of the stifling conventions of the adult world, though she's more conservative than he is and is obviously frustrated by his mercurial behaviour. She's upset when Peter steals a book for apparently no reason.

Peter's individualistic philosophy is further linked to American values by his escape plan, which consists of nothing more than hieing south of the border. It's implied throughout the film that this really isn't much of a plan. Peter and Julie never discuss what they will do when they get to their unnamed destination. These links to the United States seem to underline the juvenile, trendy nature of Peter's plans. (Incidentally, their eventual escape route is noteworthy. Joyce Nelson observes in *The Colonized Eye* that the Queen Elizabeth Way [QEW] was built in order to encourage traffic between Canada and the United States, specifically northbound. In fact, the QEW was actually built before the Trans-Canada Highway, which was intended to link the country.)[7]

On the other hand, Peter's parents are linked to the old English-Canadian order, as evinced by Mary's choice of restaurants when she tries to lure Peter back home—the aptly named "Georgian Room, Toronto's swank restaurant at that time."[8] Mary and Warren's criticism of Peter takes three forms, mostly based on rules he's broken or proprieties he's failed to adequately observe: (a) he's harassed either about his lack of responsibility or his inability to handle any, yet accorded little or no freedom—evident in his father's lecture following Peter's arrest (Peter's complaints are frequently dismissed because, as Mary tells him several times, he's only a "little boy"); (b) he's scolded for the way he embarrasses his parents (witness Mary's anger at being humiliated by a call from Peter's principal); and (c) he's chillingly dismissed as "a bad investment" by Warren near the end of the film. Mary also chides Warren that things won't "pay off" for Peter if he doesn't respond more readily to discipline. As many have noted, financial language is prevalent. It's clear that English-Canadian society as Owen presents it is incapable of dealing even with Peter's mild form of rebellion, and can only reiterate the rules he's supposed to follow.

As Harcourt notes, important battles are fought in very public spaces, as if Peter's parents and the adults around him consciously want to humiliate and infantilize him.[9] In the prim Georgian Room, Peter rejects Mary's last offer to return home; Warren harangues him in a barbershop; Peter's parole officer asks him—point-blank—if he's having sex with Julie. Everyone feels entitled to tell Peter what to do—and they frequently step beyond the bounds of propriety within which Peter is expected to live.

Despite all the talk of duty, Warren and Mary are themselves hardly paragons of responsibility. As they battle heatedly over Peter, he simply walks out the door with the keys to the showroom car. After Peter's arrest, Warren opts to leave him in jail rather than take responsibility for him. The arrest itself (similar scenes are repeated in *Partners* and *Unfinished Business*) underscores the cost of rebellion in a society that seems preternaturally incapable of responding to it. Even a minor infraction like truancy is seen as somewhat cataclysmic. Fun, no matter how innocent, is not an option. There are few if any compelling role models for Peter. Mary tells Warren he's a joke, dismissing him with "You ease out of every possible situation that comes up … Smiling Warren Mark!"[10] The rest of the adult world isn't much better. The parking-lot boss, at least initially, treats Peter like an adult—joking about sex, asking him what his concerns are, taking him to shoot pool. He gives Peter far more attention than Warren does. As Joan Fox points out in a contemporary review, "This

Nobody Waved Good-bye

man is remarkably played by John Vernon with all the suggestion of capable adult masculinity that would be so appealing to the boy."[11] Eventually, though, he tries to blackmail Peter.

Authority is strangely omnipresent and virtually omniscient at times. In a moment reminiscent of a similar scene in *A Dangerous Age*, the minute Julie comments on Peter's running a red light, the cops show up. The principal's calls are always timed to embarrass and undercut both Peter and Julie. Her mother—who's almost interchangeable with Peter's in looks and demeanour—grills Julie about where she's been in order to catch her in a lie, after the principal has informed her about Julie's truancy.

At the same time, Warren and Mary are not entirely unsympathetic. Peter is rude, selfish, irrational and thoughtless much of the time. The Marks believe they're acting in Peter's best interests, and any mistakes they make (like leaving Peter in jail overnight), usually result from frustration.

Peter is obviously quite conflicted. As others have commented, he has absorbed his parents' values in spite of himself. Note, for instance, his fascination with the showroom car his father brings home. He's as excited by it as a young child by Christmas, and is especially drawn to its power: "It must be as powerful as anything!"[12] Escape for Peter means stealing a car. (Then again, it would be hard to get very far on his scooter.)

The minute he's out on his own, Peter increasingly becomes obsessed with money. All the conversations with his boss at the parking lot are dominated by cash; the boss habitually greets Peter by asking him if he's making any money. Peter rather condescendingly lectures Julie on how important money is, then pressures her to get a job—a request that is a far cry from the quasi-bohemian, principled complaints about consumerism and middle-class complacency we've heard from him earlier. And Peter's arguments with Julie begin to mirror his parents' fights in their nastiness—and usually end with a discussion of money. When Julie arrives at his rooming house, he gallantly greets her with "What do I need a girl with a suitcase for?"[13] He operates on a clear double standard in regard to Julie, pleading with her to return to her parents' home, something he adamantly refuses to do.

Nobody Waved Good-bye

Tellingly, Peter himself never decides to pursue his interests in music beyond serenading Julie and hanging with his friends—this despite the folk boom of the period. He appears to see music as a hobby, considering it only in a slightly more positive light than his parents do. Within Owen's cinema, Peter counts as a failed or stifled artist. His only outlet is pointless acts of usually peevish disobedience.

Peter's crimes are all petty, childish and spur of the moment, typically sparked by his inability to accept any kind of discipline. He's somewhat hapless. He steals the showroom car because his parents irritate him at dinner and their ongoing rancorous argument—clearly audible from his room—makes it impossible for him to study. Following his first meeting with his parole officer, he lifts a book. He steals a car for the second time, partly because of the pressures he's under but also because his father has turned down his request for a loan. His actions are in part inspired by the lack of responsibility and freedom afforded him. He's also less than eager to enter the world of his parents, for good reason.

The film's imagery underscores Peter and Julie's transitional state. The opening sequence features the pair talking on a bridge; later, Peter walks along its railing. During an idyllic scene in which Peter and Julie take a canoe out on a lake, they pass under a bridge with several children staring down at them, harshly silhouetted against the sun. The pair is often presented as infantile, childish. Julie sporadically appears to be sucking her thumb and exhibits a marked tendency to pout; when Peter meets his mother for lunch, he orders a glass of milk and sucks on his fork. He lacks the one thing that would acknowledge his independence: a driver's licence. His father answers Peter's question about when he'll get one with a rather infuriating "Sometime." Their innocence relieves them of a certain responsibility and makes the parents (and their lack of understanding) appear bizarrely cold.

The presentation of Toronto ushers in an image that will dominate much of English-Canadian cinema for the next couple of decades: the city as a place of dread, a breeding ground of alienation and disenfranchisement. Other filmmakers, most notably David Cronenberg and, to a lesser extent, Atom Egoyan, Patricia Rozema, Clement Virgo, Don Shebib and Deepa Mehta, would play with different, sometimes more intense, variations on this theme—as would Owen himself.[14] From the very minute Peter arrives in the city, he's met with hostility and indifference—when he's not being targeted for a scam. The landlord at the rooming house where he winds up harangues him for coming too early; the parking-lot boss squeezes him. When he and Julie go out on the town they are seen in empty shopping centres or subway platforms (though this can partly be attributed to the low-budget, guerrilla manner in which the film was shot). The majority of Peter's interactions are with authority figures, most of them rather suspect or unsympathetic. The only time they're seen interacting with an equal is in the chess game with the Québécois student.

This sense of unease and disenfranchisement is buttressed by the early quasi-pastoral images of Peter and Julie playing hooky. In the opening scene—as the forlorn folk song "The Water Is Wide" plays on the sound-track—they cavort in a graveyard. During their idyll on the river, they glide past a sofa tossed in the middle of the water, which only serves to mock their dream of a life together.

The unease is further supported by Owen's decision to improvise most of the action, which results in a marked sense of tension. That process included giving the actors different parts of the puzzle. Kastner, for instance, did not know that Mary knew about Peter's truancy, nor did he know that Warren would refuse to pay Peter's bail, which results in his fairly explosive resistance to being carted away by the police officers. Both scenes resonate with a surprising amount of energy, partly because of their awkwardness. The cross-talking and rants/speeches make the proceedings very different from conventionally organized dialogue. The cameraman, John Spotton, notes in an article in *Canadian Cinematography* that this also contributed to tension on the set; at one point Kastner accidentally put Owen through a plate-glass window."[15]

The actors weren't the only ones having problems with Owen's unpredictable shooting approach. A dedicated craftsman, Spotton was often perturbed by the less-than-ideal conditions that confronted him. Owen's reason for improvising was, incidentally, exploratory: "I shot with improvisation and the reason I did was that I didn't know what it was to be English Canadian, nor did anybody else." (The technique did allow for a certain level of serendipity as well. The woman who recognized Peter in the parking lot was actually a family friend of the Kastners, captured with a hidden camera.)

Despite the freewheeling, even accidental way in which the film developed, it seems to be carefully devised, full of structural echoes. The coffeehouse chess game contrasts with the pool-hall shakedown by the parking-lot boss. Peter's parole officer and his boss grill him on his sex life. As mentioned before, references to money abound.

On his return to NFB headquarters in Montreal to own up to what he'd done, Owen received a rather stern lecture, but there was little anyone could do. In fact, he was even given the opportunity to reshoot some scenes. Then there was the editing process. As Peter Harcourt points out,

Nobody Waved Good-bye was shot like a typical Unit B production.[16] One of the philosophies prevalent in the unit (encouraged by Daly) was to shoot until you had the theme or the material you wanted.[17] This approach could become problematic with a short film, as it did with *Toronto Jazz*, and shooting a feature-length film only upped the ante. By the time the shoot was over, Owen had 75,000 feet of film; once he had a cut he was happy with and ready to show his superiors, the film had been worked over so much—had so many splices from editing—that it could barely be run through the projector. At the first screening, the sound—a crucial element in a film that relied so heavily on its realistic tone—would constantly slip in and out of sync.

The NFB remained supportive, but it was an organization that had no substantial experience in releasing feature films. The majority of its product either went out attached to studio films or though an alternative distribution system devised by Grierson during the Second World War. The critic Robert Fulford, an early champion of *Nobody Waved Good-bye*, noted, "It seems too bad that the National Film Board is bringing its latest feature into town in such an apologetic way ... It was made here with a local cast and a local director; its subject is middle-class Toronto suburban society and an adolescent's revolt. But the Film Board is bringing it here in something like secrecy."[18]

Initial domestic reviews were somewhat mixed. *The Globe and Mail's* Frank Morriss dismissed it as "dreary, ineffectual."[19] The writer and critic Germaine Warkentin praised it as "a French-Canadian film made about Ontario teenagers."[20] The film opened and closed in both Montreal and Toronto in December 1964. It didn't win the Canadian Film Award for that year—nothing did; the judges didn't feel there was anything good enough to warrant an award.

However, the film did garner significant international attention at the Montreal Film Festival in August 1964. *Nobody Waved Good-bye* might have remained in limbo were it not for an invitation to the New York Film Festival in September 1964, where it impressed critics (particularly Judith Crist of *The New York Herald-Tribune*, who considered it the highlight of the festival and later ranked it as one of the best films of the year) and Don Rugoff, who ran an independent distribution/exhibition company called

Cinema V. (In the seventies, Rugoff would distribute another landmark Canadian film, Richard Benner's *Outrageous!* [1977].) *Nobody Waved Goodbye* was released in New York in April 1965, and it met with overwhelmingly positive reviews and was featured in countless publications, including *Time, Vogue, Life, The New York Times, The New Yorker, The New York Herald-Tribune, The Washington Post, The San Francisco Chronicle, The Los Angeles Times* and later *The Times* in London.

Nobody Waved Good-bye

The international reviews normally praised the film for its documentary look, Spotton's cinematography, its performances, the vibrant, unscripted quality of its dialogue and its rough edges—which for many probably meant it was unlike a Hollywood product. In the review that in many ways established the film's place in Canadian cinema, *The New Yorker's* Brendan Gill noted that it "isn't a grim sociological study … but a story, commensurate in the purity of its intentions, and even in the artistry of its execution, with, say, *The Catcher in the Rye.*"[21]

The film was subsequently re-released in Canada and was significantly more successful its second time out. After its acclaim in New York and Canadian re-release, Joan Fox wrote a particularly blistering piece about the initial reception in Canada, linking the negative reaction to the WASPiness of the culture and its resentment at being confronted with that fact. "The great lack of sympathy which I have heard expressed for this film hangs largely around the character of the boy," she comments. "As Peter Kastner plays him, he just simply gets on the nerves of a lot of people who can't imagine themselves with such a son in the family. I think that merely indicates the incredibly philistine and smug nature of what is still the major part of English Canadian society. Why this kid is so gauche that he asks his sister's fiancé if he's really happy at the prospect of devoting his life to dentistry … Apparently nice suburban Torontonians do not do such unthinkable things."[22]

In some ways it may seem curious that *Nobody Waved Good-bye* became such a milestone in the Canadian industry. It would be a mistake, of course, to maintain that the film is independent of cross-border or international currents. The folk movement, to which Peter is attuned, was an international phenomenon, its roots firmly planted in the United States. The themes in Owen's film are not dissimilar to those in many American or international works of the period. (Many of the American and Canadian reviews, including Joan Fox's, compare it to Frank Perry's *David and Lisa* [1963].) Many countries were experiencing the repercussions of the baby boom, which created a very large mass of young people with buying power, political clout and their own tastes, nurtured by a mass media that frequently catered to their interests. It's obviously a phenomenon that *Nobody Waved Good-bye* responds to. Owen himself is as likely to couch Peter's rebellion in American terms: "It was the beginning of the sixties and that was in the air—rejecting the Eisenhower values."

Yet from a Canadian perspective, the film is radically different from other films released during the same period. Most obviously, it is clearly shot in Toronto, often at easily identifiable landmarks like the high-WASP Georgian Room in Eaton's department store, the Toronto Islands, the subway. This may seem insignificant to some, but for many who would go on to enter the film industry—as filmmakers, scholars or cultural producers—it was far from insignificant. Accounts of the sudden thrill of recognizing one's own geography are common to Canadian film audiences and enthusiasts alike. David Cronenberg frequently cites the impact that David Secter's feature *Winter Kept Us Warm* (1965) had on him when he saw it as an undergraduate at the University of Toronto.[23] (The film was made by students and shot on campus.) Piers Handling, the CEO of the Toronto International Film Festival Group, has written about the excitement of seeing Yonge Street the first time he viewed *Goin' Down the Road*.[24] Wayne Clarkson, the head of Telefilm Canada, the federal funding agency for film and television, recently commented that seeing *Nobody Waved Good-bye* in his youth was proof to him that films could actually be made in Canada.[25] As Edward Said notes in his influential essay on Yeats, "Yeats and Decolonization," "a colonized country has to repopulate its spaces."[26] One indication of the significance of this issue is that the presentation of Toronto is seldom raised in connection with Owen's subsequent features.

Similarly, the picture the film paints of English-Canadian society

Nobody Waved Good-bye: Julie Biggs, Peter Kastner, Don Owen

remains unsettling because Toronto is still a rather WASP city. As Robert Fulford wrote in 1970, years after the film's release—perhaps indicating the considerable effect that its portrait of the city had had on him—residents were shocked at just how white the city seemed: "*Nobody Waved Good-bye* was so densely Toronto Wasp in content that it produced in some of us a painful shock of recognition."[27] This may not be readily evident to non-Canadians, but the Marks' inability to express any sympathy for their son, to acknowledge his importance to them—other than as an investment—or to find any means of communicating with him seem peculiar to Toronto and English Canada. The stuffy restaurant where Mary first tries to lure her son back home, then scolds him, is an apt stand-in for the suburban milieu—or for English Canada as a whole.

Furthermore, the film's ambivalence toward Peter and his rebellion is uniquely Canadian in its diffident relationship with the United States and that nation's individualistic values. Canadians have always had a rather difficult time with ostentatious success, which is typically perceived as "too

Owen (right) directs *Nobody Waved Good-bye*

American" or just "too much." Hugh MacLennan writes about his father's suspicion of it, and while MacLennan is referring specifically to his Scottish ancestry he could be speaking for Canadians in general: "Buried in the fastness of his complex mind, was the contradictory notion that if a Scotchman ever amounts to anything important, he will not be any too real, either, for some beastie will come along and spoil him."[28] That said, it's a sentiment/superstition that makes hubris virtually impossible. (For a more contemporary example, witness the rather gleeful feeding frenzy in the Canadian press around Conrad Black's fall from grace.)

The reference to *Cleopatra*, the most notorious studio debacle of its time, seems rather germane. It was, in the days before *Heaven's Gate* (1980), the most spectacular box office failure Hollywood had ever produced, a classic example of the disastrous side of American cinematic excess.

Nobody Waved Good-bye kick-started the feature film industry not only in English Canada but also in Quebec, to some degree. Shortly after Owen completed shooting his film, Gilles Groulx would make his first feature, *Le chat dans le sac* (1964), which was also intended to be a half-hour documentary. In 1965, Gilles Carle would make one of the first major domestic Québécois hits, *La vie heureuse de Léopold Z* (also for the NFB), by claiming he was making a documentary on snow removal in Montreal, then shooting a feature instead. (It was actually supposed to be part of the same series as Groulx's film.) Indeed, Owen's ability to effectively "steal" a feature from the jaws of documentary became part of Canada's cinematic folklore. One of the subplots of Peter O'Brian's *Hollywood North* (2002) concerns a young filmmaker's scheme to finish a low-budget art movie by stealing footage from a bloated tax shelter production.

Owen would never experience quite the same degree of success in his career, though many of his subsequent features, documentaries and short films would be well received, particularly internationally. His subsequent work would continue to spark debate, but none had the impact of *Nobody Waved Good-bye*. Even in Canada, the film would be eclipsed by Don Shebib's *Goin' Down the Road*, which regularly tops polls of the best Canadian films.

There are probably many reasons for this, and a debate on the comparative merits of the two films could occupy a lot of space (and *Goin' Down the Road* is technically far more proficient), but it is worth noting that Shebib's film contains a variety of motifs to which Canadians would inevitably be more sympathetic, most notably regional disparity. As Joyce Nelson notes in *The Colonized Eye*, many of the early NFB productions practically hammered this domestic issue home.[29]

Unlike *Nobody Waved Good-bye*, *Goin' Down the Road*, with its focus on rustics being beaten down by the big city, also has a rather mythic/archetypal quality. Moreover, its two protagonists can be charming in their innocence and are extremely colourful. It represents the first time genuine Canadian hosers were seen onscreen (before the term was coined by the satirical comedy troupe who created SCTV). It also lacks the earnestness of Owen's film. In contrast, *Nobody Waved Good-bye* was about a far less colourful character and a much less colourful Toronto. As Fulford's response noted above shows, Owen may have done his job too well.

3

The Lost Canadian

Despite the protracted release of *Nobody Waved Good-bye*, Owen kept extremely busy through 1964 and 1965, working on a number of different projects, many of them overlapping. Virtually all of them play off a similar theme, exploring the lives of people who have left Canada and the reasons why. It's difficult not to see some of these films picking up where *Nobody Waved Good-bye* left off. Several focus on artists and reflect an increasing international awareness on the part of the subjects and perhaps Canadians in general.

The documentary short *High Steel* (1965), the first to be completed, focuses on Mohawks from the Kahnawake reserve near Montreal. Known for their expertise in ironwork and high-rise construction projects, they have been recruited to work on the extension of a skyscraper in New York City. As the film explains, their reputation can be traced back many decades to their building an enormous bridge across the St. Lawrence River in 1904. Based on interviews with one of the workers, Harold McComber, and with narration by Don Francks, the film records the group's experiences and the danger and difficulty inherent in the job. The NFB has had a long-standing commitment to documenting Aboriginal culture, beginning with *The Longhouse People* (1951) by Allan Wargon and stretching to the present day, as evidenced by its support of filmmakers like Alanis Obomsawin (*Kanehsatake: 270 Years of Resistance* [1993]) and Gil Cardinal (*Totem* [2003]).

High Steel

The tone of *High Steel* is exuberant, largely because of Macomber's pride in his work and the exhilarating cinematography courtesy of John Spotton. Bruce Mackay's uptempo song (it was originally supposed to be provided by Gordon Lightfoot) talks about "building mountains of iron and steel," valorizing the Mohawks' work and skill and imbuing their activities with a quasi-natural aspect. The shoot itself was rather risky, which may account for the overexcited tone. (The film crew, shooting with heavy and cumbersome 35 mm cameras, had to gain access to the construction site many storeys above the ground by climbing across a ladder from an adjacent building.)

High Steel also records the impact of modern society on a traditional culture. The film is about an exported, perhaps exploited, labour force. Economics have forced McComber to leave his rural environment to work and thus adapt to another world ("Everybody eats Corn Flakes, so we gotta eat Corn Flakes," he explains), and the film highlights his sense of alienation and dislocation, as he laments the fact that his children, already separated from their traditions, are now growing up without a father. In a key article on Owen, "Don Owen's Obliterated Environments," James Leach argues that the film explores the repressive nature of the social and economic costs of technological advances, citing the way in which a "picturesque image of the village dominated by its church is obliterated by a large ship, suggesting that technological influences have superseded the old religious ones."[1] This image also contributes to the film's sense of alienation and exile and evokes the life-is-elsewhere motif.

The film is suffused with mortality, belying its upbeat surface while reflecting the precarious status of Mohawk culture. Owen recounts through the use of archival photos that many Kahnawake Mohawks were killed in the building of the aforementioned bridge. In one of the film's more telling images, a young mother pushes a baby carriage through a cemetery. (Leach argues that this can also be interpreted as an image of renewal.)[2] *High Steel* was Owen's first crack at editing a film himself; it went on to win the Canadian Editors Award for Best Editing.

Owen's next film, *Ladies and Gentlemen, Mr. Leonard Cohen* (1965), returns to a favourite subject: art and artists. It remains one of the most appealing pieces produced by the NFB in the sixties. The film, which follows the Canadian poet/songwriter on a return visit to Montreal, was co-directed by the NFB veteran Donald Brittain. (Owen left midway through the project to work on *You Don't Back Down* in Nigeria.) The original idea of recording a tour of Canadian poets that included Irving Layton and Earle Birney was jettisoned when it was decided the other poets lacked the charisma to occupy the spotlight. Owen and Cohen knew each other socially—they frequented the same parties and shared several friends, including the NFB filmmaker Derek May. According to Owen and to Brittain's biographer Brian Nolan, Cohen moved into a hotel for the making of the film because he didn't wish to be perceived as a wealthy dilettante.[3]

High Steel

The film's narrator explains that Cohen—who at the time was living alternately in Montreal and the Greek island of Etre—often returns to his hometown to, in Cohen's words, "renew neurotic acquaintances." *Ladies and Gentlemen* opens with Cohen reading at Sir George Williams (now Concordia) University, and in the familiar, dryly humorous tone he's known for, he recounts a lengthy, absurd story about visiting a friend in Verdun's mental hospital. Eventually, he's confused for an inmate. Characterized by a voice-over as sardonic and wry as Cohen's, the film segues from the university performance with "When he's not being a stand-up comic ..."

Cohen is filmed hanging out with friends, performing, visiting old haunts (where fragments of his poems are written on the walls), jamming with musicians, extolling the virtues of the city's night life (the first act of rebellion by man, according to Cohen, was refusing to sleep), making television appearances, attending academic cocktail parties (which he dismisses as meat markets) and, intermittently, writing.

In some ways, the film is as much a record of sixties Montreal nightlife as it is of Cohen. In fact, the filmmakers clearly see Montreal as a kind of outpost within Canada where the pursuit of art and culture are viable activities. Unlike the Toronto of *Nobody Waved Good-bye*, Montreal offers both pleasurable intimacy and comfortable anonymity. Cohen is glad the town is still small enough that he knows where the night owls congregate; but he can also abandon them and wander into a cheesy movie whenever he feels like it.

Like *Toronto Jazz*, *Ladies and Gentlemen*'s presentation of the artist initially emphasizes work and the effort it takes to become an artist, showing Cohen in his hotel room scribbling madly, though the man's sensibility gives it a unique, broader spin. The emphasis is on the preservation of self against a host of oppressive influences. Cohen frequently talks about the hotel as a "sanctuary," being pursued by "hounds" and protecting and preserving a "state of grace." He's forced to meet with academics and is badgered by the broadcast journalist Pierre Berton, who looks quite miffed at Cohen's apolitical insouciance. (Fellow poet Layton seems equally anxious to speak for Cohen.) Cohen's description of his situation echoes the comments of the hipsters of *Toronto Jazz*, but both subject and film take this image of the embattled personality even further, suggesting that identity in modern society itself is a precarious construct at best and often culturally determined (the mix-up in the asylum, for instance, or Cohen reading a poem about stereotypical images of Jews).

Cohen refuses to fully cooperate with the notion that art is work, so the filmmakers shift their focus to art as play. He frequently declares that he no longer writes. The conventional notion of the tormented, serious poet is partially mocked by his interest in and comfort with pop culture. He's seen listening to pop music while writing, perusing tabloids at newsstands and wandering into a rundown theatre to watch an overtly trashy genre film, *Beyond Mombasa* (1957).

Ladies and Gentlemen...

MR. LEONARD COHEN

16mm

Black and White

44 minutes 1 second

Written and designed by Donald Brittain
Direction: Donald Brittain
Don Owen
Photography: Paul Leach
Laval Fortier
Roger Racine, C.S.C.
Film Editor: Barrie Howells
Music: Don Douglas
Producer: John Kemeny

A camera study of a poet, Mr. Leonard Cohen, 30, from Montreal but now resident in Greece. This film was made on one of his brief visits to his home city, to which he comes from time to time to "renew his neurotic affiliations", he says.

In Montreal he receives an enthusiastic reception: as a poet declaiming his lines from the stage for crowds of young people; and as a maverick member of his family where, he says, only his grandfather showed gifts similar to his own.

That Mr. Cohen has the gift of poetry is very evident from what is heard from him in this film

and from what his friends say about him. His poetry readings are principally from his recent collections, *A Spice Box of Earth* and *Flowers for Hitler*. Among the people seen with the poet is Irving Layton, a fellow poet also with a Montreal background.

The portrait presented by the film is informal. Mr. Cohen is shown walking the streets of the city, eating in a popular night spot, sleeping in his three-dollar-a-night hotel room, and even taking a bath. Wherever he is, and no matter what he is doing, there is little doubt of his primary interest in poetry and the poetic impulse.

Produced by THE NATIONAL FILM BOARD OF CANADA

P. O. Box 6100, Montreal 3, Que.

Ladies and Gentlemen can be seen in many ways as a corrective response to the NFB's celebrated *Lonely Boy* (1961), directed by Wolf Koenig and Roman Kroiter. (When *Nobody Waved Good-bye* was released in New York, it played on double bills with *Lonely Boy*.) The film explores the pitfalls of celebrity as well as its inherent artificiality by following the pop star and teen idol Paul Anka, who seems oblivious to the fact that he might be perceived as a product. In contrast, Cohen is acutely aware of his persona, evident in his decision to move into the hotel, his polished, self-deprecating performances and his wry yet romanticized view of himself. As the narrator notes, he had a reputation for dabbling and not being particularly serious. The critic George Woodcock's essay on Cohen's work suggests that he was always a pop star in training rather than a poet, citing an interview with him in which he said as much.[4] The word *con* is always used by Cohen to describe the whole artistic endeavour. Echoing the conclusion to Jean Rouch's *Chronique d'un été*, the film shows Cohen presented with rushes, then he comments on them. He's mildly troubled by what he sees and states that until then, he didn't realize "what style of man I was." At the end of the sequence, he writes "caveat emptor" on the wall of his bathroom. As James Leach notes, the film almost abandons its project of interpreting Cohen.[5] In some ways, it implicitly offers a critique of the American cinéma-vérité movement by openly dispensing with the notion that the subject isn't aware that he's being photographed. In spirit, *Ladies and Gentlemen* is far closer to the Québécois version of cinema direct.

Owen's first portrait of a solo artist, the film also represents the first time he concentrates on an artist who is at home with and successful in his chosen profession, despite Cohen's protestations. This comfort stems from Cohen's skill at juggling internal and external contradictions, or to paraphrase him, the balance with which he rides the chaos around him. He's a radically different protagonist from *Nobody Waved Good-bye*'s Peter Mark, perhaps because of his sense of humour—or maybe he's a Peter Mark who's actually succeeded, though, like Peter, Cohen is apolitical, and both have uneasy relationships with their parents. Cohen's meeting with his mother is a stiff, formal affair, somewhat reminiscent of a similar scene in Jutra's *À tout prendre*. (The film's narration, perhaps engaging in some image-making of its own, constantly stresses that Cohen and his family are estranged.)

Cohen's persona in the film and in his performances is one of the first examples of the bemused, distanced and put-upon Canadian artist-intellectual, a trope that has been revised and reborn many times, most recently in Don McKellar's filmmaker-chauffeur in *Childstar* (2004). Part of Cohen's evident comfort may come from his status as an international transient. Prior to the sixties, Canadian artists felt themselves misfits in their own country, as much of Owen's cinema illustrates. Cheaper and more accessible international travel and the occasional international success (which Owen experienced with *Nobody Waved Good-bye*) opened up other possibilities. Owen's next effort, *Monique Leyrac in Concert* develops this international theme further.

Made for the CBC's *Telescope* series, *Monique Leyrac in Concert* is one of Owen's liveliest, freshest films—due in no small part to Leyrac's own vibrancy and zeal as a performer. This vitality is heightened by the unique nature of the singer's particular art form, that of cabaret singing, which demands that the performer be equally adept as an actress and as a vocalist. Leyrac was successful in several formats, including recordings (she specialized in releases devoted to individual composers) and one-woman plays (focusing on subjects like Sarah Bernhardt). But her talent was probably best realized in solo performances. At the time Owen made this portrait, Leyrac was at the height of her career, having recently released her version of Gilles Vigneault's "Mon Pays" ("My Country"), an unofficial anthem that not only became her signature song but also helped solidify Québécois' own awareness of theirs as a distinct cultural entity.

The film meets Leyrac as she returns following triumphant performances in Europe and is designed to introduce her to English-Canadian audiences, principally by stressing how successful she is internationally, either by showing recent performances or by comparing her to recognizable, better-known international figures. "If Édith Piaf is France, then Monique Leyrac is Quebec," explains the host and narrator, Fletcher Markle. The comparison also imbues her with an iconic, representative status. Owen records Leyrac as she shuttles between performances and also recounts her arduous, painstaking preparations to present a new song.

The film concentrates on three central issues. First, it shows Leyrac as a distinctly modern woman, vastly more independent and career-oriented than her predecessors.[6] Her agent, Samuel Gasser, may play an important role, but she is in complete control of her work and presumably her career. As she claims in the film, "I do it all myself." In rehearsals, she appears to have high expectations of her musicians, frequently stressing the need for perfection: "All the technique must be perfect." This drive is seen to be both exemplary and novel. Leyrac also confides that she has little or no choice in her rather hectic schedule. As she puts it, "If I stop work … I will die." These statements of course echo or pick up motifs from Owen's other portraits of artists, including the notion of the artist as a craftsman, art as a demanding profession, artists as addictive personalities. Almost entirely absent, however, is the notion of play. Leyrac is probably as unlike Leonard Cohen as one could possibly imagine, at least in the way she presents herself and her dedication to her craft.

Second, Leyrac represents the shift in Quebec society from the way it was during the repressive and hyper-conservative Duplessis regime to the more liberal period of the Quiet Revolution that followed. Leyrac specifically cites the lack of opportunities and proper theatrical venues fifteen years previous—conditions essential to her field. (The full force of her artistry would only be evident in a theatrical setting, as opposed to, say, nightclubs. Her powerful performance at the end of the film rather spectacularly demonstrates this.) Owen inserts a number of shots of the Quebec countryside, invariably blanketed in snow, with farmers diligently battling the elements, people skating and even a sleigh ride. The montage both exults in the exquisite imagery and implicitly criticizes this stereotypical image of Quebec (think of *Les raquetteurs*). The sequence seems like a flashback to another time, a postcard image.

Third, the film debates the inherent tension between Leyrac's roles as an iconic figure who represents Quebec culture and a singer/performer in her own right, worthy of comparisons to other artists working in the same field. The debate is instigated by Leyrac herself. She's not sure whether it's necessary for the songs she performs to reflect Quebec's realities, which she refers to as problems. Her assertion that her work "is not only a local thing" opens up into a subsequent discussion about how a performer doesn't necessarily get lost in a role; he or she is giving a performance first and foremost. She essentially refuses the representative status assigned to her. The climactic performance of "Mon Pays" seems designed to illustrate this point, stressing the power of her art by example.

The universalist note may seem distinctively, self-effacingly Canadian, but it also underscores themes evident in works like *High Steel* and *Ladies and Gentlemen*, which stress Canadians' interaction—and place—in the world, and our ability to perform/compete on that level. Owen would of course have been familiar with this after his own success in New York. As mentioned earlier, the need for Canadians to justify themselves internationally first and domestically second is especially pervasive in the film industry but not unheard of in other fields (not only is life elsewhere, but so is validation). Leyrac's international success itself is trumpeted perhaps to justify English-Canadian interest in her since, presumably, if she were "only" a Québécois star she would be of little significance. Her prominence also underscores the fact that Quebec, unlike English Canada, has never shied away from celebrating its own performers or constructing its own star system.

Unlike the Cohen film or *Toronto Jazz*—in which the artists were valorized for their refusal to be defined in social or conventional terms—*Monique Leyrac in Concert* politicizes culture, or at least acknowledges the political aspects of culture. However, Leyrac is not an individualist like Peter Mark or, for that matter, Leonard Cohen. Her importance derives from both her representative status and her skill. This relatively unambiguous acceptance of one's cultural roots is rare within Owen's body of work.

Owen's next short film—the one that dragged him away from the Cohen project—was made for the NFB. Titled *You Don't Back Down* (1965), the film looks at a young couple, Alex and Anne McMahon, who were sent from Canada to eastern Nigeria to aid in the country's modernization efforts. As the narrator, John Vernon (Peter's sleazy boss in *Nobody Waved Good-bye*), informs us, Nigeria is experiencing "the itch of modernity." The contrast between industrialized, modern Canada and Nigeria is established in the opening shots, which present a variation on a familiar Owen motif: shipyards and docks, except that here tankers are replaced by large canoes. The McMahons are there as part of CUSO (the Canadian University Services Overseas), the Canadian version of the United States' Peace Corps.

You Don't Back Down is primarily about culture shock. As Vernon explains, "Two years in Africa may leave the McMahons questioning their own assumptions." Owen concentrates almost exclusively on Alex, a physician who's in charge of establishing and operating a local medical clinic. The challenges are legion, including lousy equipment, poor sanitation, suspicion and reluctance on the part of the locals, inadequately trained staff and poverty. Patients are required to pay a fee, something Alex complains about to no avail. Moreover, the McMahons have to deal with their own inexperience both as professionals (Anne is a teacher) and as inhabitants of a country whose ways are extremely foreign to them.

The film recounts the day-to-day experiences of Alex as he struggles to provide health service for the area. (Anne's work is only mentioned in the film, partly because of her reluctance to participate.) Alex is rather reserved, even stuffy, most of the time: at one point he responds to a botched operation with "Oh, heavens." And he's not exactly lovable, often berating the nurses for their incompetence and usually speaking to the patients as if they weren't present. During a dinner with Anne Williams, a Peace Corps teacher from Arkansas, Alex is amused by her accounts of her students' writing assignments, one of which comments on her long nose. He responds with "They write so spicy, so frank," a remark that seems weirdly colonial and condescending. Still, he's extremely diligent, running off in the middle of the night to perform emergency surgery.

You Don't Back Down

The biggest struggle for both Alex and Anne is homesickness and their inability to understand or function in the local culture. Alex confesses, "When you come over here, you're really ignorant … so suspicious of everything." The most oft-repeated comment centres on their desire to return home. Anne seems even more at odds with their environment than Alex. She confesses that "the first time I tried to cook alone ended in tears." After Alex is called away on an emergency during the dinner with the Peace Corps teacher, Anne leans over and whispers how much she hates it there.

The most revealing moment, however, comes when Alex discusses his greatest fear, that he will "face a challenge and I'll have to back down. But you don't back down. You just can't." This comment, which comes almost immediately after the emergency operation mentioned above, refers to doubts about his own skills as much as cultural conflicts.

You Don't Back Down

It would be entirely unfair to judge the McMahons exclusively by our standards, and Owen emphasizes the exotic nature of the environment and the McMahons' inability to achieve isolation or genuine involvement. The leper colony for infants, for example, is right outside their kitchen. Festivals and celebrations go on constantly, but the McMahons are seldom involved, the lone exception being when Alex sits down to a more formal meal with a visiting politician. Intriguingly, instead of trumpeting the McMahons' efforts or successes, *You Don't Back Down* focuses on their inability to cope with their new environment. The film is less about success than alienation, more about personal bewilderment than triumphant colonialism, and fuses the traditions and approaches that influenced Owen earlier in his career; its tentativeness echoes the work of Unit B while its awareness of the pitfalls of colonial responses is reminiscent of Rouch's films.

For his next short film, *A Further Glimpse of Joey* (1967)—he once described it as a kind of warm-up for his feature *The Ernie Game*—Owen took a break from documentary and world travel.[7] The film is set in Toronto with a script written by Tanya Ballantyne, with whom Owen would later collaborate on *Notes for a Film About Donna & Gail*. Nine-year-old Joey (Shaun McNamara) has recently been adopted by a middle-aged couple, who are having a very difficult time dealing with his tendency to wander off alone without any notice. Prior to his adoption, he was transfered from one foster home to another, and there's a rather explicit suggestion that he was physically abused at some point.

The mother, Sheila (Norma Renault), is a bit of a worrywart, but she's understandably concerned. Much of the time she's seen on the phone, expressing her distress to her husband, Paul (Sean Sullivan), who's far more sanguine about Joey's disappearances. Joey in fact behaves like a troublesome teen who feels he has the right to do what he likes without any explanation. But he's astonishingly independent, so in the early going we tend to accept Paul's take on the situation. (Joey is something of a variation on *Nobody Waved Good-bye*'s Peter, with privation and possibly abuse replacing bourgeois dictates.)

Most of the film concentrates on Joey's peregrinations. He definitely gets around, wandering about the waterfront, boarding the subway and ending up one day at the Royal Ontario Museum. (He's particularly taken with dinosaurs.) The film shares some similarities with David Secter's second feature, *The Offering* (1967), which also boasts protagonists who appear determined to experience the entire city.

At the museum, Joey meets an older man who notices that he's dropped his pocket knife and returns it to him. The older man befriends the boy, buying him an ice-cream cone and telling him about his own son, who lives on the West Coast. It's difficult to read this situation. It's hard not to see the friendly stranger as potentially dangerous (child abuse was infrequently reported at the time, so public awareness was not as acute as it is now), but he could simply be showing concern for Joey. The other adults who notice him, including an elderly woman, react by glaring at him. The older man's friendliness, though, certainly feels out of place in the WASP Toronto of the time. The city itself is presented as a cold, sometimes sparsely populated place, its inhabitants oddly unconcerned about a young boy wandering around alone.

53

That said, the man is far more adept at drawing Joey out than his adoptive parents, mainly because he relates to Joey on his level. In contrast, Sheila and Paul are more perturbed by Joey's inability to acknowledge rules and regulations than by whatever is motivating his disappearances. They're not that different from Peter's parents: At one point, they even openly wonder whether adopting the boy was a mistake. Throughout the film, Joey is silent about what may or may not be bothering him. He's obviously lonely—witness the scene where he's overjoyed to meet an old friend, who promptly leaves him behind, or his tendency to exaggerate to try to impress people. There's also his near-obsessive whittling; he's almost never seen without a piece of wood and his jackknife. Like those of the failed artist Peter Mark, or later Ernie, Joey's attempts at self-expression are seen as odd or problematic.

The film climaxes with a dispute between Joey and his parents that ends with Paul spanking him, which seriously displeases Sheila, who complains, "He's been hit enough in his life." Joey promptly packs his suitcase, drags it downstairs and tells them he's leaving. The situation is defused when Sheila engages for the first time in a conversation with Joey, reminiscing about her own attempts to run away. There's actually real affection among the three of them, though the footage accompanying the end credits, showing Joey roaming about once more, clearly hints that he will continue to do that. Like many of Owen's films, *A Further Glimpse of Joey* is decidedly open-ended. It is easily one of the filmmaker's more forlorn works. The conclusion implies that Joey won't grow out of this behaviour for quite a while—and that his parents are ill equipped to deal with the situation. An even more downbeat version of *Nobody Waved Good-bye*, the film shows a distance between Joey and his adopted family that seems greater than the gap between Peter and his parents. Owen's next two projects, *Notes for a Film About Donna & Gail* and *The Ernie Game*, would concentrate on adult characters even more alienated and lost than Joey. In fact, with its rambling structure and lost hero, *Joey* could indeed be an early draft of *The Ernie Game*.

Ernie's Song
Don Owen

I am the Lion's wound, the anger
of a dazed and dying world—
eyes, eyes these points of hunger
see men strangers all minds wild.

Shrill is the voice I speak with, soft
the mind's voice, the heart's murmur,
always the tongue remembers only
the stinging blood, the nerves murder. Living

to walk toward the spirit's window
my mind alert. Here, wounds heal,
eyes see, like a new dawn's shadow
your light upon my darkness falling

A city is a magnet that pulls in many young-
sters like Donna and Gail, girls from smaller places who find work in factories or
shops. Often they live alone, in a room
rented by the week, eating sandwiches,
French-fries and cokes, making out. But
sometimes two of them will get together
to ease their expenses and their loneliness.

notes for a film about Donna and Gail

16mm   Black-and-White
Screening Time : 48 minutes 38 sec.

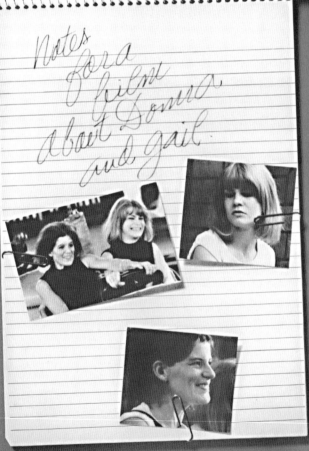

This film is a character study of the
two girls, showing the currents that
brought them together, revealing
the differences in their natures, the
contradictions that first attracted
them and finally drove them apart.
And because it induces thought about
the nature of loneliness and the in-
completeness of people generally,
the story of Donna and Gail reflects
in some degree the situation of anyone who has shared the life of someone else.

By representing himself as the ob-
server and appearing to piece together what he knows or guesses of
the girls' story, the film-maker en-
courages the audience to do the
same, and even to engage in a wider
interpretation. It is a film that en-
grosses and involves the viewer and
persuades him to hang onto the story
by talking about it afterwards. It is
as though the film were, in fact,
notes about Donna and Gail from
which something larger is bound to
develop.

Direction : Don Owen
Production : Julian Biggs
Camera : Jean-Claude Labrecque
Editing : Barrie Howells
Script : Gerald Taaffe and Don Owen
Cast :
Michele Chicoine, Jackie Burroughs
Supporting Cast :
John Sullivan, Aino Pirskanen,
Evelyn Gordon, Ray Bellow,
Gino Marrocco, Derek May

Produced by
The National Film Board of Canada

4

Undun

Owen's next two films, *Notes for a Film About Donna & Gail* and *The Ernie Game*, show him at his creative peak and, not coincidentally, his most adventurous. Like *Nobody Waved Good-bye*, these films are portraits of alienation and disenfranchisement in large cities, with Montreal replacing Toronto. The shift in setting is crucial, altering the nature of the protagonists' alienation. The near-sociological, documentary emphasis of *Nobody Waved Good-bye* is replaced by more universal and possibly more fundamental concerns. Instead of focusing on a holdout from the WASPy, materialist middle class, Owen concentrates on issues that separate his protagonists in less culturally specific ways, including class, gender, sexuality and mental illness. The central figures in both films are outsiders, divorced from the culture in which they're trying to survive, mirroring Owen's own outsider status in Quebec.

The medium-length work *Notes for a Film About Donna & Gail* recounts the brief friendship between two working-class women. It represents a radical departure not only for Owen but for English-Canadian cinema as well. Conventional accounts of English-Canadian cinema in the sixties have always stressed the period's realist and documentary impulses or a combination of the two, exemplified by *Nobody Waved Good-bye* and Don Shebib's *Goin' Down the Road*; Allan King's two seminal documentaries *Warrendale* and *A Married Couple*; Larry Kent's series of films outlining the rifts in middle-class values, including *The Bitter Ash* (1963) and *When Tomorrow Dies* (1965); Irvin Kershner's adaptation of Brian Moore's novel *The Luck of Ginger Coffey* (1964); and to a lesser extent, David Secter's two features shot in Canada, *Winter Kept Us Warm* and *The Offering*. (In fact, the debate on realism as a viable option for a cinema still struggling to find itself occupied much of the critical discourse in the seventies.)[1]

In contrast, *Notes* persistently resists verisimilitude and is clearly influenced by contemporary European cinema, especially the work of the French New Wave and Jean-Luc Godard in particular. Like Godard's *Vivre sa vie* (1963), *Notes* is divided into chapters, a technique that both unsettles the viewers—by reminding them they're witnessing a construct rather than reality—and, in the process, highlights the issue of representation itself.[2]

However, the Godardian inflections seem less central than the use of a highly suspect narrator, who, from the outset, admits that he's uncertain whether he even knows the basic facts—and is fully aware that he may be projecting his own reality on his subjects. In fact, Owen's method of distancing his audience seems more typically Canadian. The film seems like a parody of earlier NFB films, especially in their use of supremely assured voice-overs and their claims that they represent reality. The visual look (it was shot on 16 mm black and white) and some of the staging of the scenes invoke documentary, only heightening the viewer's uneasiness in interpreting the material. Its subject is equally as radical for the time, for the film deals with what may or may not be a lesbian relationship between Donna and Gail.[3]

The film is based an idea by the Montreal journalist Gerald Taaffe (a former editor of *The Montrealer* who shares the scriptwriting credit with Owen). As Owen recalls, "He told me, 'I've been writing an outline about these girls. I don't really want to write a script yet, but I'll give you some notes,' so he wrote something called 'Notes for a Film About Donna and

Gail.' I thought that's a great idea; we'll turn it into a film. I had the idea that *Notes* would be very, very tentative, and to keep it like that. I think that's the thing that makes me most proud of the film—the sort of elusiveness of the structure; it's like deconstructing narrative in a sense because it questions how you would know somebody. You can't [even] in your personal life ever really know another person. The narrator backs away from saying certain things, and it does have a little bit of that *Rashomon* ambiguity of character. It was kind of improvised, although there were script references. [The assistant director] Tanya Ballantyne and I wrote a script, [but] I didn't really even look at it while I was shooting."

Notes for a Film About Donna & Gail opens with a row of young women riding up an escalator. The escalator seems to be floating mid-air. It's an anonymous, alienating effect, suggesting that the city is effectively being fed a new crop of young women, all of whom resemble one another. The unseen (and uncredited) narrator, Patrick Watson (later a prominent TV personality and author), recalls the first time he met the wistful and enigmatic Donna (Michèle Chicoine) at a coffee shop.

He's immediately sexually attracted to her, specifically commenting on her sensuality and beauty, but he's also troubled by the fact that he can't really figure her out. He's acutely conscious that he may be projecting qualities onto her. A shot frames her in a window staring out at the rain, a device that romanticizes her and underscores his need to categorize her. One of the reasons why he cannot come to grips with her character is that she's an inveterate liar, claiming, among other things, that she's a student and that her wealthy father doesn't permit her to work. Actually, she's from a working-class family in Northern Ontario, though even these basic facts remain up in the air by the end of the film. As Watson notes, she seems to half believe her own fabrications. Each time she tells a lie, the image freezes almost imperceptibly, as if to reflect the narrator's doubts about her stories.

When she gets a job at a garment factory, Donna meets the far more assured and aggressive Gail (Jackie Burroughs). Gail realizes that Donna's having difficulties with the machines and helps her out, thereby becoming a mentor of sorts. Soon enough they become inseparable, moving in together, even wearing matching outfits. Periodically, they discuss moving out west—a return of the escape or life-is-elsewhere motif from

Nobody Waved Good-bye—though this idea seems far more important to Gail than Donna. Slowly, Donna grows more stable; her fantasies seem less outrageous the more she hangs out with Gail. Perversely, the narrator laments this development: "Was Donna changing or was my attitude toward her changing?" He later adds, "I couldn't help feeling uneasy. Their relationship had entered a new phase, and an outsider could only guess what it was."

Notes for a Film About Donna & Gail

The implication in these early scenes is that Gail is a predatory lesbian taking advantage of innocent, troubled Donna, a notion supported by the fact that she wants to whisk her away to other cities. There's a strong suggestion that the relationship between the girls is sexual—they wrestle in bed and engage in pillow fights—but there's very little definitive evidence of anything sexual going on between them. Their behaviour as it's reported reflects male sexual fantasies as much as anything else: it's highly unlikely that the narrator, presumably the source of our knowledge, could know what the girls do when they're alone in their apartment. It seems improbable that last evening's pillow fight would come up in conversation with someone they hardly seem to know. And Watson's narrator often confesses that he simply doesn't know them very well. His uncertainty destabilizes our response to what we're seeing, encouraging us to doubt what's being presented to us on virtually every level, since the ostensible source for the story can't really know what he claims to know.

The most significant rupture with conventional realism, however, comes when the girls visit an amusement park and two men hit on them. The more loquacious one, Gino, urges the girls to trust him because a relative is a police officer. Eventually, they accept a lift from the men, but Gino abruptly stops the car and tries to make out with Gail. She resists and angrily gets out, demanding that Donna (who's far more interested in the man she's with) come with her. Gino defuses the conflict by coaxing Gail back into the vehicle.

Later on—in a chapter introduced by the intertitle "An Alternate Version"—the narrator fortuitously meets Gino, who tells a very different story. He claims that Gail did not get back into the car and that the three of them drove off without her. In the tradition of macho men whose virility has been maligned, Gino concludes that Gail simply doesn't like men.

Unable to determine which of these accounts is true, the narrator moves on, relating that the factory boss (Sean [credited as John] Sullivan) fires Donna because of her poor work, habitual lateness and lousy attitude. She provides a bad example, he explains, and she'll only inspire others to mess up. (Of course, there's also the possibility that he's uncomfortable with the girls' close relationship.) This forces Gail to quit as well. In many ways, this is the turning point in the film, as Gail's act can be interpreted as predominantly selfless and the repercussions of her decision invert the power dynamic.

Notes for a Film About Donna & Gail

The girls respond to their dismissal by leading the wild life—staying up till all hours (echoing Cohen's claim about the first act of rebellion in *Ladies and Gentlemen*)—until the money starts to run out and Gail begins to look for a job. She eventually finds one selling records at a Kresges department store. Donna doesn't take their financial situation very seriously, preferring to stay at home and sleep. This infuriates Gail, who's supporting them and doing all of the chores; at this point, it's not Gail but Donna who's in control. (In some ways, the narrator's version of their relationship prefigures *The Bitter Tears of Petra von Kant* by Rainer Werner Fassbinder in its portrait of power struggles in a hidden relationship, though it's far less rancorous.)

In a scene set in a laundromat, Watson basically interviews Gail about her relationship with Donna. Mocking both the notion of "knowing" another person and the documentary format, he first asks the most basic question: Where is Donna really from? Gail explains that Donna simply isn't capable of taking care of herself: "She doesn't know too much about how things are, how you gotta be," says Gail. Donna is growing more and more petulant, trashing their room one morning for no particular reason. Gail returns, sees the shape the place is in and leaves without saying a word.

The narrator decides that he may have been wrong all along. The heroine of his story may actually be the sensible Gail, who does her best to aid Donna. Gail is photographed far more sympathetically as the film proceeds and the narrator's opinion of her develops. This is linked to her burgeoning relationship with a Québécois man and the possibility that she might be sexually interested in the narrator. After all, his presentation of his first encounter with Donna is highly sexualized, and here he explains how Donna responds readily to his compliments while Gail is slightly more suspicious and less easily conned—implying that he's been making overtures to her as well. Owen shoots Gail from above in the laundromat interview, making her look far less imposing than in previous scenes. Part of this shift in our perspective may also be attributed to the casting of Jackie Burroughs, whose looks can vary instantaneously from harsh and unsympathetic to striking and inquisitive.[4]

Curiously, the only character whose integrity isn't truly called into question is Gail. The account of the night at the amusement park is explicitly identified as a joint narrative told by both girls, perhaps because they cannot acknowledge their exclusive relationship. Still, the level of uncertainty in the film is so intense that you're left wondering why Gail's claims aren't questioned in the same manner as the narrator's or Donna's.

The film ends with the narrator relating several different versions of what happened to each woman. Donna may have inherited a lot of money from an uncle in Spain or moved back to Timmins; Gail either became a dress designer or moved out west.

63

Notes for a Film About Donna & Gail

Owen plays out conventional, male-generated fantasies and stereotypes about lesbians and female sexuality, which are effectively dismissed by the narrator's inability to determine the truth. Each of the girls is stereotyped. Donna is irresponsible, flighty, sexually promiscuous and naive enough to be preyed on. She is frequently seen as childish. In addition to the tantrum mentioned above, she's especially fond of Bobo, her stuffed animal, which even Gail teases her about: "He's so stupid. Gee, you'd think you were four or something." By the end, though, Donna is seen as very troubled and completely incapable of caring for herself. At one point, Gail discovers a bottle of prescribed pills. (There's a similar discovery in *The Ernie Game.*) Donna's tears after Gail's departure in fact suggest that the relationship was more important to her than to Gail, or, at the very least, more than she initially let on.

Gail is sensible, experienced, harsh and—in the early section of the film—predatory. Toward the end, though, she comes across as being more maternal, caring for Donna rather than exploiting her. That said, at certain points both Donna and Gail are associated with childhood and play, like Peter and Julie or some of the artist figures in *Toronto Jazz* and *Ladies and Gentlemen*. James Leach argues that Donna's childish view of the world changes Gail's perspective, but Gail's view of social conventions isn't that much more complex or mature than Donna's.[5] Witness the laundromat scene where she tells the narrator that they dress alike because they want to show that they're "wild."

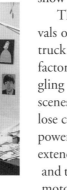

Notes for a Film About Donna & Gail

They are usually seen in playgrounds, carnivals or playing in the spray from a street-cleaner truck (immediately after they're fired from the factory). Owen frequently presents them giggling and chasing each other. In many of these scenes, they are in situations where they either lose control or are about to, echoing the sense of powerlessness in the opening image. There's an extended sequence with the pair in bumper cars, and they're also seen whizzing down some sort of motorized slide. On the one hand, these scenes acknowledge the girls' vitality; on the other, they underscore how directionless they are. They're almost infantilized, which only makes their situation—or at least Donna's—seem more hopeless. There's a level of pathos that echoes Peter Mark's ham-fisted attempts at rebellion.

The girls' claustrophobic, exclusive relationship provides a haven, but it also guarantees their isolation. They are customarily seen alone in strangely barren spaces, much like Peter and Julie. The girls' only outside relationships involve money (the factory boss and their landlady) and sex (Gino, the narrator and Gail's male friend)—in other words, two potential forms of exploitation. As in *Nobody Waved Good-bye* and later *The Ernie Game*, the landlady/landlord here is seen as a demanding, unsympathetic figure—a representative of the hostile outside world—telling Gail that if the two of them stay in the room, they'll have to pay more rent (perhaps because she wasn't keen on their living together).

The creepy, voyeuristic narrator only intensifies the impression of isolation and danger. His obsessive interest in the girls is unusual, to say the least. It's almost as if he was stalking them. Watson's flat, reflective reading makes him seem even more suspicious. (Owen discarded an earlier version of the narration, read by the NFB house writer/narrator Stanley Jackson, because Jackson's more mature-sounding voice made the character sound too voyeuristic.)[6] When initially approached by Taaffe with the idea for the film, Owen felt that Taaffe's interest was primarily voyeuristic. Later, people would complain that the narrator was simply a stand-in for Owen.

Owen has said that the women represent different halves of his own persona, with Donna the imaginative and immature half and Gail the practical and realistic. He has said that the film "expresses my own particular kind of schizophrenia—my teeter-tottering between two worlds."[7]

Ironically, *Notes for a Film About Donna & Gail* again got Owen into hot water at the NFB—this time because it *wasn't* a feature, which is what he was expected to produce. That wasn't the only irony. The film was actually taken away from him at one point by the director of production, Julian Biggs (whose daughter starred in *Nobody Waved Good-bye*). When nothing happened with the film, probably because of the film's decidedly idiosyncratic structure and tone, Owen was put back on the project. The film won a prize at the Montreal International Film Festival for medium-length works in 1966 and a General Information Award at the Canadian Film Awards in 1967.

Notes represents Owen's first significant attempt to address the issue of mental illness, though he touches on the subject in both *Ladies and Gentlemen, Mr. Leonard Cohen* and *A Further Glimpse of Joey*. It becomes the ostensible subject of his next feature, *The Ernie Game* (1967), though his interest in it appears to be as much in its metaphorical possibilities as the actual condition. Conceived as a Centennial project (1967 was Canada's hundredth birthday) and co-produced by the CBC and the NFB, *The Ernie Game* was intended to be part of a trilogy that would be screened on television and then released in theatres. The finished film, however, probably wasn't exactly what either institution had envisaged.

Very much a product of its time, the film—which centres on wild-haired Ernie Turner (Alexis Kanner), a bisexual would-be writer, full-time transient and former male hustler—represents the most drastic fictional

vision of the artist as disenfranchised figure in Owen's work. Ernie is the least governable character in Owen's cinema, incapable of responding to any discipline or routine. This madman-artist-hero who opposes conformity recalls Ken Kesey's novel *One Flew Over the Cuckoo's Nest*, with its asylum-as-society metaphor. And the film owes an intellectual debt to R. D. Laing, a psychoanalyst who argued that the excessively repressive nature of Western society only validated the actions and beliefs of those it rejected, or considered insane; Laing also valorized the less repressed, intuitive behaviour of children. At the same time, the film is decidedly divided in its view of Ernie; on some levels, it's a nightmare vision of the artist as a madman, a fraud, a sham and an enigma. Indeed, the entire film courses with ambiguity and ambivalence.

Owen's first feature in colour, *The Ernie Game* effectively sums up the director's career to date, recalling much of his previous work. It mixes formats and genres like *Notes for a Film About Donna & Gail*, combining slapstick comedy and parable with a thorough anatomy of mental illness. There are structural echoes of *A Further Glimpse of Joey*, whose lost and incommunicative hero spends his time wandering the streets aimlessly, similar to Ernie. The title connotes both play and scam, evoking Cohen's comments about art and persona being a con game in *Ladies and Gentlemen*. And like *Notes*, *The Ernie Game* is partially about how difficult it actually is to know someone, but this is less a central theme than a result of Ernie's troubled mental state and his representative function as an artist. Similarly, the film's approach to narrative invariably keeps the viewer guessing as to exactly what's going on. Scenes tend to erupt with little in the way of set-up. In its own way, *The Ernie Game* is as unreadable as *Notes*. Like Peter Mark before him, Ernie Turner provokes a wide variety of contradictory responses.

The opening shot shows Ernie staring out the window of his flat at a group of kids playing nearby. After a few desultory hacks at a typewriter, he strolls over to the mirror to admire himself and worry about his pimples. He's interrupted by his landlady, who demands he pay his rent immediately.

Ernie promptly jumps out the window, suitcase in hand, and takes to the streets, hitting on the first woman he encounters. Unfortunately, she's

Québécoise and doesn't understand what he's saying. This counts as the only instance in either *Notes* or *The Ernie Game* where language becomes an issue, and serves to emphasize the abstract nature of Owen's presentation of Montreal as a stand-in for any city. (Owen does refer to the significance of the separatist movement at the time through the inclusion of "Vive le Québec libre" graffiti in a shot later in the film.)

After trawling the streets for someone who will react to him, he meets

The Ernie Game

Donna (Judith Gault), clad in an outlandish red wrap with matching hat. (Both Donna and Gail appear in the film as the hero's competing love interests/substitute mother figures, though the relationship with the former incarnations is tangential at best.) She's intrigued by him, though she suspects he's a drunk because of his shambling pace, lugubrious demeanour and general lack of direction. He tells her he's a writer and, when asked what he writes about, responds with "Girls." She invites him to her place and he confides in her, telling her, "I'm queer. I've been attracted to some men."

A weird sixties-style bit of dance/foreplay/slapstick/game of hide-and-seek follows, sans dialogue, and accompanied only by exuberant rock music. The sequence suggests the Marx Brothers or silent comedy bits like the oft-repeated routine of people charging in and out of different doors and continually missing one another. (The link to silent comedy is buttressed by a picture of Chaplin in Donna's bedroom. Chaplin's tramp of course represents the most romanticized outsider figure in early American cinema.) This sequence reflects Donna and Ernie's playfulness, but it also suggests Ernie's mood swings and hysteria. They almost have sex, but Ernie's mood suddenly shifts and he rebuffs her. In a reflective, post-coitus-interruptus moment, he explains that he's often considered himself a saint, someone "who knows that everything is the same—who knows that there are no differences."

On the subway, he encounters Max, an old friend from his hustling days, who invites him to a house party. Owen actually explains the relationship through a quasi-interview, much like the narrator's interview with Gail in the previous film. At the party (which perhaps provides a glimpse of the parties where Owen, Derek May and Cohen met), Ernie picks up a pretty blonde, insults another for wearing too much eye makeup, then retires to the living room when his ex, Gail (Jackie Burroughs), enters. He confronts her and asks why she didn't visit him in the hospital. Gail tells him, "You're disruptive and you make everything chaotic and ridiculous" and explains that that isn't what she needs at this point in her life. The Chaplin connection is revived when Ernie picks up a cane and wanders around the party with it.

The Ernie Game

Ernie sits down in the living room to listen to Leonard Cohen playing the film's theme song, "The Stranger," to an entranced and silent group. The song, as James Leach points out, describes Ernie almost perfectly. Like the song's dreamer protagonist, he "wants to trade the game he knows for shelter."[8] Ernie's need for attention and taste for disruption—or maybe just his disagreement with Gail—overcomes him before Cohen finishes the song. He moans loudly and leaves the room, with everyone staring at him. Reaching the doorway, he glares back, prolonging the moment. Gail charges after him, and they head back to her apartment, where she resists Ernie's pathetic demands that they sleep together.

After a day of wandering around the streets (and walking right past Donna without even acknowledging her, probably because she's talking to another man), he sneaks into Gail's apartment through the second-floor window. Later, she checks in on him to see if he's done any writing, which he hasn't. Gail commiserates with him, commenting, "Maybe you're not a writer. Maybe you're a plumber or something." The statement implicitly connects Ernie's behaviourial problems and his artistic ambitions, which in Gail's eyes prevent him from becoming a useful, functioning member of society.

On the street again, Ernie is approached by a tourist with a camera and asked to take a picture. He treats the photo as if it was a fashion shoot, clicking away endlessly and wasting the poor woman's film. Showing up at a community centre, he speaks to an exasperated social worker, who greets him with "What is it today, Ernie?" He explains that he wants to have a real life, i.e., a middle-class existence, and no longer wants to be a case study/patient. After some coaxing, she agrees to lend him her new typewriter, which he promptly pawns for a camera. This won't be the first time

The Ernie Game

that those who should respond to Ernie's problems either give him short shrift or get conned. He wanders the streets, overjoyed by the attention the camera inspires, whether it's hostile or welcoming. Significantly, there doesn't seem to be any film in it.

Ernie moves in with Donna and her son and comes close to leading a "normal" existence. This bliss is short-lived, though, as he quickly lapses into depression, refusing to get out of bed. Donna grows more and more frustrated. Perhaps speaking from experience, she tells him that he can get himself out of his funk simply by looking at things differently. Ernie dons a three-piece suit and tries to make a living as a door-to-door salesman. He's a disaster at it and, after being rebuffed a couple of times, steals a car and takes off. This development is totally unprepared for and utterly unreadable. Is this Ernie's fantasy/hallucination or does it actually happen? He has no money, so it's doubtful he could buy a suit (or that he owned one previously), and we never see him go out for a job interview. There is, of course, the possibility that he's simply play-acting. The job he sees himself in doesn't differ too much from his regular behaviour, and allows for the maximum amount of attention *and* rejection.

Donna finally asks him point-blank if he'll ever be able to support her and her son. Echoing Gail's complaint earlier, she tells him that if he cleans himself up maybe she could fall in love with him. They quarrel, and it turns physical, with Ernie eventually pulling a gun on her. She leaves, and Ernie fires at his own image in the mirror. Later, he meets Steve, a suspi-

Shooting *The Ernie Game*

cious American, who first tries to pick him up, then agrees to help Ernie in his plan to carry out a robbery. The first attempt (the target is a movie theatre) is a disaster because Ernie refuses to follow through. They regroup, and Ernie successfully robs a convenience store but insists on bragging about it in a bar. They scuffle in a nearby alleyway, and Steve takes his cut and runs off.

Ernie sneaks into Donna's apartment and swallows an entire bottle of sleeping pills. He makes several phone calls, looking for any kind of attention—including one to his shrink, who ignores him—then calls Donna, pleading for help. (At first, he thinks he's calling Gail.) In the final shot, he stares out the window at a group of kids playing in a fenced-in schoolyard with the Canadian flag fluttering in the background.

The Ernie Game offers a fairly detailed account of mental illness. (Owen was inspired by the lack of knowledge about the lives of the mentally ill.)[9] The arc of the narrative follows Ernie's inevitable decline as he shuts out everyone around him and winds up alone and suicidal. Owen catalogues a long list of symptoms: mercurial mood swings, a reliance on fantasies and lies, delusions of grandeur, depression, catatonia and suicidal urges.

Throughout the film, Ernie is subject to near-schizophrenic, intensely erratic mood shifts. In addition to suddenly and perhaps unaccountably rejecting Donna (while in bed, he first tells her he hates her, then expresses his love for her), he stomps out from a meal Gail makes for him—into the dead of winter—for no apparent reason.[10] And of course there is the failed robbery attempt at the cinema, where he just grins foolishly when Steve expects him to pull the gun on the theatre manager and his staff. When confronted with his failure to do anything, Ernie simply laughs wildly.

Alexis Kanner in *The Ernie Game*

He's an unconscionable liar, much like the previous film's Donna, concocting a variety of wild stories to get attention, invariably relying on dramatic scenarios. On the day he meets Donna, he talks about his dying stepfather, then recounts his father's death, which he turns into a grisly joke about the undertaker switching his father's head with one belonging to another corpse so Ernie's father could be buried in a suit. At another point, he tries to persuade Donna to let him into her house by telling her that his mother has suddenly died. He shows up with presents for Donna's son, claiming he stole them all. Donna speaks for most viewers when she says it's impossible to know if he's lying or not. His lies are completely inconsistent, which indicates his precarious mental state more than any strategy beyond an immediate need for attention. When Donna visits him to see if he's okay after his mother's alleged death, he tells her that she's perfectly healthy and wonders where she got this information. Ernie's lies are accompanied by delusions of grandeur—he believes he's fundamentally different from other people, in fact a saint. "I wouldn't be so much trouble if I weren't a genius," he tells his social worker.

Like a small child, Ernie never acknowledges anyone else's potential commitments or responsibilities. He calls in sick for Donna when he wants her to stay home and whines when she leaves for work after he

Shooting *The Ernie Game*

moves in with her. Similarly, he's extremely upset when he sees either her or Gail speak to another man. He nearly explodes when he sees Donna walking home with someone else; he creates a disturbance at the house party where he first encounters Gail after she enters with another man. When Donna cuts his hair, he breaks down in tears.

Ernie's lies often centre on his mother and his family—and he sees both Donna and Gail as potential mother figures, seeking shelter from them and relying on them to take care of him. He tells Donna that he's attracted to her because she's the kind of woman he wanted his mother to be. This need is complicated by Ernie's sometimes virulently sexist attitude to women. In his eyes, Donna is a repressive, demanding mother who insists he look after her, *and* a whore, capable of cheating on him or abandoning him at any time. (Given Donna's promiscuous behaviour, his suspicions aren't unrealistic.)

Ernie is also seriously prone to depression. When he and Donna eventually move in together, he responds by lying in bed all day, much like Donna in

The Ernie Game

Notes. At certain points, such as when he's waiting for Gail to bring him the meal she's cooked, he seems almost catatonic. Following his final major battle with Donna, he visits a library and begins telling a young woman a parable about a man who dreamed he was a butterfly. The woman he's speaking to (rather logically) departs midway through the story, but Ernie continues on, nonplussed. The story itself describes his fragile mental condition; the hero wakes up unable to determine whether he is a man dreaming that he's a butterfly, or a butterfly dreaming that he's a man. Like Ernie, the subject of the tale is losing his ability to distinguish between reality and dream/fantasy.

Toward the end of the film, beginning with his final quarrel with Donna, Ernie becomes increasingly psychopathic and violent, slapping Donna, threatening her with a gun, shooting his own image in the mirror, then engaging in some rather lackadaisically committed robberies. His refusal to take these activities seriously again indicates his inability to separate fantasy from reality.

The Ernie Game

A classic pathological narcissist, Ernie is driven by self-hatred as much as self-love. Much of his time alone is spent in front of the mirror, shifting from admiration to self-criticism to disappointment to self-loathing. In the opening scene, he seems to be admiring himself, then complains about his complexion. Eventually, he kisses his reflection. After his quarrel with Donna he shoots at his image in a mirror. These scenes emphasize Ernie's self-absorption but also his disappointment and disgust with himself. Away from the mirror, Ernie relentlessly seeks attention and recognition, but he seldom distinguishes between rejection and acceptance. When he disrupts Cohen's song, and the entire party is glaring at him, he turns and glares back, revelling in the attention despite its hostile nature. When he actually receives attention, he's completely unsettled by it, an index of his self-hatred. After their initial meeting, he tells Donna that she must be odd since she spoke to someone like him on the street. Later, he tells Donna that he isn't used to getting attention and therefore has no way to respond to it when he does receive it, though it's difficult to accept this at face value, given his predilection for falsehoods and his skill at special pleading.

Yet Ernie is far more than just a case study. Indeed, Owen suggests that this sort of response is inadequate when Ernie complains about being identified as a case study when he visits the social worker, and expresses his desire to become a real person, not simply a patient. His joke about his father's burial on one level mocks psychiatry and undercuts Donna's comment that Ernie can snap out of it simply by changing his perspective. (This is decidedly ironic, given Donna's behaviour in the previous film.) Ernie isn't able to simply switch heads and make himself presentable; his problems run deeper than that.

Ernie also represents Owen's quintessential failed artist as well as a radical break from his earlier portraits or defences of artists. Gone are the equations of art and work. Depending on how you look at him, Ernie is a failed artist or, worse, a fraud. He tells everyone he's a writer, though we never see him really working; outside of his listless typing in the opening scene and his futile attempt to write in Gail's apartment, he's mostly seen wandering the streets. He rather pointedly leaves behind his typewriter in the first scene, even though you would assume this was his most prized possession. After convincing the social worker to lend him a typewriter, he promptly pawns it for a camera and wanders about taking photographs of people— remaining the centre of attention at least for a brief period of time. Revising the con-game image first mentioned by Cohen in *Ladies and Gentlemen*, Ernie is also a petty criminal, which equates art with outcasts and the underworld, though hardly in any romantic way. Ernie's crimes are as inept as Peter Mark's.

Here madness and infantilism replace the other explanations for artists offered in films like *Toronto Jazz* and *Ladies and Gentlemen*—underlined by Owen's conflation of Ernie's stories and his life. Ernie tells Donna that he's writing a story about a man who has just been released from a mental hospital. Later, during a conversation between Gail and Ernie, we find out that he has just been released from some kind of hospital. Ultimately, Donna rejects him by throwing his stories at him in the middle of the street, linking his problematic behaviour with his art.

Ernie's artistic pretensions are associated with his infantile and apparently unquenchable need for attention. He justifies his existence through other people's acknowledging him. There's a telling moment in the opening sequence where he believes a woman is watching him through a window, which (as he says out loud to himself) must mean that he's interesting. Ernie's delusions of grandeur are linked to his writing. Saints and geniuses are, for some, synonyms for artists.

The familiar Owen equation of childhood, play and art is presented in far more negative terms than in previous films. In fact, Ernie's inability to distinguish between play-acting and reality becomes increasingly dangerous for him and others, demonstrated when he waves the gun at Donna and in his belief that the robbery is a lark. Instead of being charmingly childlike, he's turned childish and somewhat menacing.

Ernie is Owen's nightmare version of an artist—if not of himself. Ernie was, in fact, patterned after the author of the original stories, Bernard Cole Spencer, though Owen was again criticized for the "autobiographical" nature of

The Ernie Game

the film. (Actor Alexis Kanner does wear an ensemble that resembles Owen's normal choice of clothes at the time.) The film elicits comparisons with the equally negative portrait of an artist in Jutra's *À tout prendre*. Whereas Jutra presented himself as a cowardly bourgeois vacillator, incapable of risking anything, Owen presents the artist as an infantile fraud, driven by a need for attention.

Recalling the final scene of *Nobody Waved Good-bye*, Ernie's moment of self-definition comes when Donna demands he take some responsibility and initiative, which he refuses to do. His behaviour deteriorates following this break with Donna and becomes increasingly criminal, culminating with the robberies. Indeed, Donna and Gail serve as socializing influences.

Ernie is the consummate outsider, that status underscored by his countless surreptitious exits and entrances. Throughout the film, he leaves and enters through windows, or is asked or forced to use the back door. Ernie never really owns or occupies a space he can call his own, which

The Ernie Game

echoes the transient, temporary homes of Owen's other protagonists, including Peter Mark, Donna and Gail, Joey and even documentary subjects like the McMahons, Harold McComber, Leonard Cohen and Monique Leyrac. Society is unable to meet him on any terms, which recalls the hostility expressed toward artists that is evident in *Toronto Jazz* and *Ladies and Gentlemen*—but it's a far more venomous strain here.

Ernie is more than homeless, he's either unwanted or perceived as an embarrassing, discomfiting presence by almost everyone he meets, much like an insightful artist who tells people things they don't want to hear. Gail abandons him in the hospital and rejects him immediately when they encounter each other at the party. This rejection is, of course, couched in middle-class terms. According to Gail, Ernie makes everything ridiculous, and what she really needs and wants is someone to take care of her. His artistic ambitions are seen as irrelevant and disruptive by Gail and eventually Donna. He's ignored even by those who should help him, including his social worker and psychiatrist. Visually, he's constantly framed in mirrors, windows or empty hallways, trapped or abandoned. Ernie's bisexuality, of course, only reinforces his outsider position. There's as much pathos in his situation as Peter's or Donna and Gail's in the previous film. And like them, he's fairly clueless. Even worse, both Donna and Gail are relatively bohemian—Donna is a copy writer while Gail is a designer; Ernie is even being rejected by those on the margins.

His childish perspective is presented ambivalently; it's not simply depicted as destructive. Both Donna and Gail are drawn to him partially because of it, and he injects an energy and excitement into their lives— witness the first, failed seduction scene with Donna and the wild, exuberant play that precedes it; similarly, there's Ernie's anarchic, comic ability to turn objects and functions on their heads. When first kicked out of his apartment, he tries sleeping in a dryer at a laundromat; he turns a simple request for a photograph into a bit of street theatre. His stories similarly overturn and mock conventional perspectives.

As the film illustrates, based on the way people treat Ernie, conventional society considers artists as mild, temporary amusements, not to be taken seriously for any period of time. Ernie is an object of desire for Donna because of his eccentricity (she doesn't even mind his rather sporadic attention to personal hygiene) and because he doesn't abide by middle-class rules, though ultimately she rejects him for the same reasons that Gail does—he's not presentable and is too chaotic. In the final fight in their apartment, she tells him that people have been too good to him, permitting him to get away with his behaviour for far too long. In other words, he simply needs to grow up, an assessment that is woefully inadequate, whether we see Ernie as a madman or an artist.

Part of his collapse may be attributed to the decline of his creativity, which inevitably impacts on his self-image. He is no longer able to write. He's not a saint—in fact, he's not special at all. One could see the entire film being driven by an artist's fear that he's lost his talent or never had any to begin with. Ernie seems even more adrift than Peter Mark because his rebellion has no clear origin, no background. He doesn't even have an enemy that he can recognize, even one as vague as consumerist society. There's nothing to rebel against except himself, and Ernie is ill-equipped

Don Owen with fellow director Robin Spry in 1977

to understand himself. The closest he gets to identifying his needs and problems comes in the session with the social worker, but his refusal of any responsibility, even for his own actions, precludes this. As he tells Donna, in one of his more spectacular acts of special pleading after she criticizes him, "My personality just hasn't had a chance to develop."

It's difficult not to see Ernie's situation as a parallel to Owen's own problematic status in the film industry. Like Ernie's, Owen's interests were not specifically regulated or defined. He alternated between fiction and documentary, creating a body of work that was not easily categorized. His films were reasonably well received critically but usually commercial failures, a serious problem in an art form that demands a certain level of monetary investment from the outset.

As James Leach observes, "Ernie is an artist without a vocation."[11] No one can read Ernie's writing. The only sense we get of what he might have written is in the joke about his father's burial and the fable about the butterfly. Neither of the audiences for either tale understands their import. Donna dismisses the burial story as a joke; the woman in the library walks away before Ernie's even finished. (Anecdotes, of course, are not recognized as a major art form.)

Once *The Ernie Game* and the second of the three-part series co-produced by the CBC and the NFB, Ron Kelly's *Waiting for Caroline*, were screened on television, a scandal erupted in Parliament. New Brunswick Senator Fournier denounced them as "indecent, immoral and repulsive."[12] The third film was never made. In Fournier's defence, it must have been somewhat startling to see the two most venerable filmmaking institutions, both recipients of extensive public funding, choose to celebrate the country's centennial with a film about a bisexual hustler and petty thief. Regardless of how you feel about *The Ernie Game*, you have to admire Owen's chutzpah.

Many of the more important critics in the country defended or even championed the film, including Robert Fulford and Wendy Michener. In *The Toronto Daily Star*, Fulford praised the film's adventurous "open-mesh filming" while in *The Globe and Mail* Wendy Michener deemed it "nothing less than the best English-Canadian film to date—strikingly original."[13] It went on to win both the Best Director and Best Film prizes at that year's Canadian Film Awards, and it would play in competition at the Berlin film festival, but Owen himself would not get to direct another feature for almost a decade. According to the institutional hagiographer Gary Evans, the film's failure and Owen's provocative statements about his battles with the NFB over the making of it incited the bureaucracy. As he explains, "Angry NFB managers made sure that *The Ernie Game* was the last major work Owen did for the NFB."[14]

Seen now, *The Ernie Game* is somewhat dated, most notably in the wild dances that punctuate Donna and Ernie's attempts to make love. (It's very much a sixties film.) Yet it remains as aggravating and intriguing as its principal character, and it is one of the few English-Canadian films from the period that is genuinely personal and adventurous. In fact, one could argue that it was one of the last English-Canadian examples of a personal film that pushed narrative and aesthetic boundaries until the mid-eighties, when the Toronto New Wave and the Winnipeg Film Group emerged.

The Ernie Game

Starring: Alexis Kanner, Judith Gault and Jackie Burroughs
Direction and Scenario: Don Owen · Producer: Gordon Burwash
Executive Producer: Robert Allen · Photography: J. C. Labrecque
Music: Kensington Market · Eastman Color · An NFB-CBC production

Printed in Canada 1968

5

A Bunch of
Lonesome Heroes

Perhaps in an attempt to reinvigorate himself following the traumatic experience of *The Ernie Game*, Owen embarked on a series of films about art and artists, mostly for the CBC. The first project, *Gallery: A View of Time*, was commissioned by the Albright-Knox Art Gallery in Buffalo, New York, one of the most respected arts institutions in the United States. Its reputation was (and is) based on its architectural design—a synthesis of neo-classical revival and modernist—and its substantial collection. Judith Crist, the New York critic who championed *Nobody Waved Good-bye*, referred Owen for the job.

Though essentially a promotional piece and only eleven minutes in length, *Gallery* is one of Owen's richest short films, demonstrating that he learned his lessons from Tom Daly extremely well. It's a formal tour de force, boasting a dizzying array of techniques, including an elaborate soundscape and a startlingly wide variety of camera movements and editing strategies. In the course of showcasing the gallery's collection, Owen also offers capsule histories of art and patronage as well as evolutions in subject matter, artistic technique and the role/presence of the artist.

The film shuttles between works of art, mostly shown chronologically, and exterior views of the gallery. The method of presentation varies from distant shots of the objects to close-ups over black backgrounds (with the camera zooming in so the works seem to be approaching the viewer) to still shots of certain pieces "framed" by other works of art. In the sequences where he frames pieces, Owen places a painting between two sculptures, then changes the work in the centre, each flashing briefly on the screen. (Less frequently, he pans across sculptures placed before black backgrounds.)

In some cases, the camera movements are specifically designed to emphasize certain aspects of a particular work: for instance, a tracking shot of Alberto Giacometti's *Man Walking (Version 1)* (1960) underscores the impression of movement in the sculpture by travelling in the opposite direction from which it seems to be "moving." It looks as if the sculpture is passing the viewer (suggestive of the way that Owen changes style according to subject). Later in the film, he introduces two different modes of presentation: a slide projection and a screening of the earlier sections of the film in the gallery's cinema, presented at an extremely accelerated speed.

The soundscape is initially structured around footsteps, suggesting a viewer touring the gallery. These footsteps speed up or slow down at times, most notably when the "viewer" rushes down a staircase, pausing to eye Morgan Russell's abstract *Synchrony in Orange: To Form* (1913–14). Initially, the gallery is utterly unpopulated, and the only sound effect is the lone, implied viewer, but as the film proceeds, we begin to hear crowd noises. At first, these appear in the background, and the camera (presumably representing the perspective of the viewer) searches for the source.

In addition, Owen includes music and sound effects serving a variety of other purposes. In the first section of the film (following a tracking shot of the steps leading into the gallery), we see Cycladich sculptures (*Figure of a Woman*, [c. 2800–2100 BC]), followed by Egyptian work (including a relief fragment of *King Akhenaten Worshipping the Sun God* [1376–1362 BC]). This sequence is accompanied by electronic music and ominous bells in the distance, suggesting how remote this sensibility is from our own but also imbuing the proceedings with an almost religious aura. The exterior views of the gallery are accompanied by screeching traffic sounds, including cars backing up, which further contribute to the impression that the gallery is silent and cathedral-like. Later, when Owen takes us on a tour of the Op art section, we hear a gunshot and see a piece constructed of neon that suggests a target.

Structurally, the film begins with early religious and totemic pieces, as mentioned above. These are followed by Greek and Roman works, stressing the civic function of art and an interest in the perfection of the human form, both in presentation and subject. The chronology jumps more than a thousand years to focus on medieval, Renaissance and post-Restoration works, and we see a concomitant shift in subject matter, with commissioned portraits (like Jacques-Louis David's *Portrait of Jacques-François Desmaisons* [1782] and Sir Thomas Lawrence's *Portrait of Miss Rosamund Crocker* [1827]), beginning to outnumber the religious and civic works.

Subject matter changes yet again when we reach the Impressionists, and includes landscapes, still lifes and artist self-portraits dominating. As the section progresses, the work becomes less representational, as illustrated by several Picasso works from the first decade of the twentieth century, then increasingly abstract, with pieces by Fernand Léger (*Smoke* [1912]) and Wassily Kandinsky (*Fragment 2 for Composition VII* [1913]).

Owen moves to the theatre/auditorium for a selection of largely American post–Second World War pieces, some presented like slides projected to an audience. This section includes action paintings such as Jackson Pollock's *Convergence* (1952), colour-field pictures such as Mark Rothko's *Orange and Yellow* (1956) and collages such as Robert Rauschenburg's *Ace* (1962), which features pop culture detritus. A recap of works—with the paintings flashing very briefly on the screen—plays with chronology, juxtaposing Edward Hicks's *Peaceable Kingdom* (1848) with *The Annunciation* by Giovanni di Biondo (c. 1367) and Fernand Léger's *Village in the Forest* (1914). As the sequence develops, the symbols of pop culture/capitalist society—perhaps typified by Andy Warhol's celebrated work with Campbell's Soup cans, *100 Cans* (1962)—dominate, then the focus shifts to Op art, with its emphasis on unusual materials (like neon), technology and perception experiments.

Owen turns the implication of this sequence, the diminishing contribution of the individual artist's hand, on its head by emphasizing the work and craftsmanship in his own film, by including himself, his cameraman and his crew in several shots. When the camera tracks across a sculpture in the courtyard we see the shadow of the dolly, then the crew itself. We then experience George Segal's sculpture *Cinema* (1963), which features a figure placing letters spelling *cinema* on a movie marquee, and the camera reappears. The first presentation of Lucas Samaras's *Mirrored Room* (1966)—a small labyrinth consisting entirely of mirrors—concludes with Owen's reflection in the glass. On one level, this structure also suggests that film is the culmination of a logical development of artistic forms—or at least a synthesis of previous art forms. This possibility is supported by his gradual inclusion of and emphasis on the viewers. The only viewer in the early part of the film is the presumed one on the soundtrack. By the end, that one is joined by large groups of children and other visitors.

The inclusion of larger and larger audiences as the film progresses stresses the role that galleries play in democratizing art, and indeed, the film as a whole is an overt celebration of this role.

After *Gallery*, Owen retired to the countryside for a few years in order to care for his children while his then wife travelled. The CBC then recruited Owen to shoot portraits of three artists in several countries; all were made over a period of three months for *Telescope*, the series for which he shot *Monique Leyrac in Concert*. (It opened with the memorable line, "Now it's time to be entertained and informed with *Telescope*.") Similar to the style of the Unit B work of the fifties and sixties—in other words, unscripted and candid—the films are quite straightforward artists' portrait. Two of the projects—*Richler of St. Urbain Street* (1970) and *Snow in Venice* (1970)—were telecast. The third, *Coughtry in Ibiza* (a portrait of Owen's longtime friend, the painter Graham Coughtry), was reportedly very impressionistic. It was rejected by the CBC and never completed.

Richler of St. Urbain Street focuses on the celebrated Canadian novelist/satirist Mordecai Richler, then best known for *The Apprenticeship of Duddy Kravitz* and a resident of the London suburb Surrey. The portrait raises a familiar theme in Owen's cinema: the artist as craftsman and artisan.

Richler constantly stresses the importance of work, and the first camera movement, an elaborate tracking shot, swoops through his house and stops in his office, the central location. He specifically mocks the "artistic temperament" early on in the film, noting that he's never met an artist who maintained he had such a thing and produced anything of merit, perhaps providing a gloss on *The Ernie Game*'s hero. He also comments on how humdrum his day-to-day life is, consisting largely of work and looking after his children. Owen stresses the domestic nature of Richler's life by shooting scenes of the family at dinner, shopping for groceries and following the author as he takes his children out for ice cream.

Richler explains that his writing is not rigorously thought out in advance: "It would be quite boring to come up here [to his office] if you know what's going to happen." Instead, "I don't structure it from chapter to chapter … It just comes." The film concludes with a long shot of Richler working on his most recent book, *St. Urbain's Horseman.*

One of the subjects unique to these two portraits is the Canadian artist as exile. Owen addresses Richler's decision to leave Canada, and the role the country still plays in his work. He states that he's increasingly impelled to return home because, in his view, it's seldom that an artist experiences anything fundamental after a certain age, making his formative experiences in Canada central to his work. "There is a danger of being cut off," he confides. "That's why I keep returning to Canada." Like Cohen before him, he's forced to renew neurotic acquaintances. (Unlike him, Richler specifically discusses his exile status according to its impact on his work. Cohen's absence seems far less complicated.) The piece implicitly refutes the life-is-elsewhere notion played out in *Nobody Waved Good-bye* and *Notes for a Film About Donna & Gail.* By his own admission, Richler cannot shake off the influence of his Canadian childhood. Indeed, his decision to relocate has only made him an exile/outsider in England; as he says himself, "I'll always be a foreigner here. Still am." Ironically, his children are as embarrassed by his Canadian accent as he was by his parents' Yiddish accents when he was growing up in Montreal.

It's tempting to draw parallels between Owen's and Richler's careers. Richler courted controversy, angering both the Jewish community and the WASP establishment, and as the *Telescope* host, Ken Cavanaugh, notes, he has been dismissed as a "writer of dirty books." Owen himself was denounced for his subject matter (*The Ernie Game*) and merely for attempting to make feature films (*Nobody Waved Good-bye*). Similarly, as Robert Fulford and Richler's publisher, Jack McClelland, say in the film, Richler is famous for including his friends in his work, much the same way as Owen offended people with the supposed autobiographical aspects of *Notes* and *The Ernie Game*. Moreover, the focus on domesticity mirrors Owen's own lifestyle at the time. Finally, Richler's unplanned writing method resembles Owen's own use of improvisation.

Snow in Venice chronicles a trip to the Venice Biennale by the avant-garde artist/filmmaker Michael Snow, whose work represented Canada there in 1970. Like the Cohen, Leyrac and Richler films, *Snow in Venice* demonstrates that Canadian artists are successful and well respected abroad. The film is essentially split between interviews and images of Snow and his wife, the artist/filmmaker Joyce Wieland, as they tour Venice. Owen begins by exploring the art-as-play theme, concentrating on Snow's theory of art as a game and later citing Snow's oft-repeated comment that he makes up the rules of the game, but when he begins to lose he changes the rules. As the film underlines, he works in many forms, from jazz to photography (the exhibition at the Biennale comprises a series of photographs), from painting to film, but he also works in genres that don't, by conventional definition, exist. He describes a proposed sound piece that resembles a child's game and consists of gibberish.

Similar to the participants in *Toronto Jazz*, Snow refuses to accept any type of categorization (he seems almost camera shy), tentatively confessing that he's a painter, because calling himself an artist "just gets me into trouble." Owen shows Snow at work on a new project, using a Polaroid camera and shooting himself shaking his head so his image will be out of focus in front of famous Venice landmarks such as the Bridge of Sighs. The work (eventually titled *Venetian Blind*) is presented as playful (Snow and Wieland are like excited kids with a new toy) and innovative, particularly in his choice of tool: a popular instant-image camera.

Like Richler, Snow was then an expatriate (living in New York). He complains about corruption and the immorality of the American political structure, which narrator Cavanaugh specifically links to the Vietnam War and the killing of students at Kent State. Snow argues that the artistic or bohemian life is exemplary, as evinced by the hippie movement, which he sees as an offshoot or copy of the bohemian/beatnik ethos. For him, the artist is admirable because he has no need for the kind of power that may threaten others. *Snow in Venice* represents probably the first explicit discussion of politics in Owen's films. Cohen, Peter Mark and even Ernie Turner were largely apolitical. His subsequent work would broach the subject far more frequently, the most notable examples being *Partners* and *Unfinished Business*.

Fittingly, Owen followed the two *Telescope* segments with his only uncomplicated and upbeat fictional piece on a budding artist, *Changes* (a k a *Subway or Spain*) for the CBC's *To See Ourselves* series. Though written by Anthony Lee Flanders, it is entirely thematically consistent with Owen's other films.

Changes follows Jerry Mitchell (Frank Moore), a subway train operator for the Toronto Transit Commission, who's bored by his job but doesn't quite realize it. He's playful and rather flirtatious, stopping his train at an inappropriate moment to let an attractive woman get on, much to the chagrin of his crusty supervisor. Owen provides us with a bleak portrait of the straight world Jerry is about to reject when he visits his insurance company to renew his insurance for his car. The office looks out on a depressing, suburban landscape in winter. The employees appear to be terminally bored, and Jerry is shuttled from one floor to the next before he's sent to the right person. During the meeting with his agent, he stares vacantly and absent-mindedly out the window. On one hand, the point of the scene is how dull bourgeois life is, but it's also about the financial obligations a conventional lifestyle forces a person into—obligations that make it difficult to choose a different path.

When he helps a petite blonde carry a heavy case to a dance studio, Jerry is introduced to a new world. The woman, Helene (Elaine Werner), is taking flamenco lessons. Jerry is immediately entranced by the music. He begins taking lessons with the guitarist who accompanies Helene and finances the purchase of a very expensive guitar by selling his beloved car. One of the reasons he wants to change his lifestyle is his romantic/sexual interest in Helene. As he tells his best friend, Hank

(Zalman Yanofsky, from the sixties pop band the Lovin' Spoonful), he's just "an ordinary guy" and a princess like Helene is out of his league. (This "class division" is mocked by the fact that we see her working as a waitress.) By the end of the film, though, Jerry is as interested in playing flamenco guitar as he is in Helene. He's so obsessed with learning the complex fingering involved that he is completely distracted during work, forgetting to open the train's doors at a station. Rather than be reprimanded by his boss, he simply tosses away his cap and literally dances off the job. As Jerry's teacher tells him, "Flamenco's about more than music."

Cowboy and Indian

Changes contrasts the staid nature of middle-class existence with the energy of bohemian and artistic life, and it also represents a shift in Owen's perspective on Toronto and the changes occurring in the city itself. The increasingly multicultural character of the city is represented by the flamenco studio and the presence of Hare Krishnas on Yonge Street. In the opening sequence, we see several subway passengers (perhaps would-be writers) scribbling in notebooks in the background. As in *The Ernie Game*, art, sex and rebellion are linked, but here Jerry's romantic interests are less significant than his awakening to a different kind of life and his discovery of self-fulfillment. There's a fairy-tale aspect to the proceedings, not in tone but in structure: the film inverts the Snow White story, with Helene waking Jerry from his sleep.

Owen delved further into the changing nature of Toronto in his next film, the forty-five-minute documentary *Cowboy and Indian* (1972). Like *Notes for a Film About Donna & Gail*, it is a portrait of a friendship, this time between two Toronto-based painters/jazz musicians, Gordon Rayner and Robert Markle. Owen shuttles between Rayner's flat in downtown Toronto and Markle's farm in the country, just outside Holstein, Ontario. The film is one of Owen's final explorations of the art-as-play motif, and certainly the most raucous and exuberant. It's been called the most expensive home movie ever made[1] and mostly consists of dinner parties, booze-

Cowboy and Indian

ups, jam sessions and just goofing around. Like *Snow in Venice*, though, it accommodates the idea that work can be play.

The subjects were central figures in the lively Toronto art scene of the sixties and seventies. Rayner is a well-respected, self-taught painter whose works alternate between abstract and figurative; Markle (who died in 1990) was best known for his erotic paintings of women. His work was prominently featured in a group show that was shut down by the morality squad in 1965, largely because of his contributions. Both Rayner and Markle were part of the stable of artists shown by the dealer Avrom Isaacs at his Isaacs Gallery on Yonge Street, just north of Bloor. Isaacs was first persuaded to start a gallery in 1955 by two young Ontario College of Art students, Michael Snow and Graham Coughtry. Coughtry was one of the regulars in the Artists' Jazz Band, along with Rayner, Markle and several others.

Cowboy and Indian

A warm, appreciative portrait of Robert Markle and Gordon Rayner, Toronto artists and art teachers whose friendship and camaraderie film-maker Don Owen pictures as a defense "against the numbing Canadian winter".

Rayner, with his handlebar moustache and craggy face, represents the cowboy of the title. Markle, a heavier, more introspective man, is the Indian – part Indian, he says, "the better part". Rayner plays the drums enthusiastically, enjoying the gestures as much as the sound; Markle fingers the keys of his electric piano gently. It is the rapport between the two that attracts Owen – that, and the ambience of their situation, at Markle's farm or Rayner's apartment in the Spadina Avenue "little Europe" of Toronto.

There are women in the film. Markle speaks admiringly of his wife, and she is often in the scene. But women are peripheral in this study; it is masculine friendship that Owen illuminates, both in what he shows of the two men and in what they say about each other. He shows them in the city, teaching in the art school, listening to jazz or playing it in a downtown tavern. At home they bring out their paintings and each in his way explains what he likes, what he is after.

Both men are nearing their middle years, a time when ordinarily the boisterous friendships of youth crumble under the attrition of time, domesticity, ambition. Yet with these two the companionship continues, mellows, shores up their enthusiasm for life. In their pleasure in each other's company, in shared joys of art and music, and memories, they are holding the winter's numbness at bay. That is what this film communicates in this friendship between "cowboy" and Indian.

Direction and Editing: Don Owen
Assistant Director: Paul Saltzman
Photography: Doug Kiefer
Assistant Editor: Sandy Altwerger
Location Sound: Jim Jones
Sound Editing: Bill Graziadei
Re-recording: Roger Lamoureux
Producer: Tom Daly

16mm   Color
Screening Time: 44 minutes 59 seconds

Produced by
The National Film Board of Canada

Distributed by
The National Film Board of Canada

National Film Board of Canada
P.O. Box 6100, Montreal 101, Quebec

Printed in Canada   106C 0172 033

The playfulness of the principals is evident everywhere in *Cowboy and Indian,* especially in the way that they insist on acknowledging the camera's presence. Rayner attacks the lens with a paintbrush and speaks to the crew. During a dinner sequence, Markle demands that the crew be allowed to eat as well. Both the opening and closing credits are unconventional. Rayner begins writing the opening credits in the snow (presumably in Toronto) with spray paint; Markle completes the job at his farmhouse. Owen recites the closing credits in voice-over. All this business brazenly contradicts the tenets of cinéma-vérité and the *Candid Eye* school. In fact, Owen frequently and blatantly includes himself in shots (most notably during a sequence where they're rearranging the instruments in Markle's farmhouse studio), making the work closer to the Québécois version of direct cinema, with the filmmaker very explicitly implicated in the proceedings.

The title evokes the childhood game, but refers specifically to Rayner's cowboyish behaviour—and his love of Westerns—and Markle's Mohawk heritage. He describes himself as the only Mohawk who's afraid of heights. (Both his brother and father were high-steel workers.) The title also conjures up American frontier stereotypes, which the film is devoted to overturning or at least satirizing. In place of the traditional notion of two contrasting and opposing cultures, Owen shows us two colleagues with mutual interests. The dated nature of the opposition myth is satirized in the music in the film's opening scenes, a free jazz riff on Hollywood musical standards invariably used in connection with Indians.

In contrast to such clichés, Owen offers a uniquely Canadian frontier myth via a story Rayner relates about the ghost of the legendary painter Tom Thomson, which, according to Rayner's anecdote, still canoes around Northern Ontario. Thomson, who died in 1917 under mysterious circumstances in a lake in Algonquin Park, was a

Cowboy and Indian

Don Owen's drawing of Robert Markle

friend and associate of the artists who would in 1920 form the Group of Seven. Their fresh and vivid style of landscape painting, somewhat Impressionistic, caught the imagination of Canadians. Thomson's influence on Rayner is evident (he goes on at length about Thomson's singular brushstrokes). The myth of an artist's ghost haunting the regions where he painted effectively replaces the American frontier myth. The film also represents an evolution in Owen's own perspective on the artists' place in Canadian society: instead of outsiders who need to be defended and justified, artists can be seen to embody a national ethos.

Cowboy and Indian offers a portrait of an increasingly cosmopolitan Toronto that allows artistic communities to thrive. Besides the sequences with the Artists' Jazz Band playing at a tavern, there is a decidedly homey scene with Rayner waving across the street to two people in an apartment above Gwartzman's, a popular art supply store. This sense of community even extends to work: one of Rayner's most novel creations is an ongoing project called *Charlie's Books*, which he hauls out at one point. The notebooks were often worked on communally by several artists, including Coughtry and Markle. The jazz band itself represents a collaborative effort, as does the film.

Through his sporadic voice-over, Owen also rejects several outsider stereotypes of Canada, noting that Canada is not a winter wonderland for those who live in cities. He describes the film as a "survival kit" for those preparing for a long Canadian winter. *Cowboy and Indian* also sets up oppositions between city and country, only to dispel them. On several occasions, Owen transports us from the city to the farm (and vice versa) by beginning a pan in one location and dissolving to the other midway through. Since the scenes we encounter are virtually identical, regardless of location, we sometimes barely notice the transition. This conflation

REMARKLEABLE

Don Owen

Hoisting a Molson with his left derrick
Head thrown back to laugh
(chins ascending the staircase)
whose presence is very much present
bulky and witty, obscene grace
Mohawk brave in the wilds of the Twenty-Two.

Our token Indian on the warpath
Pursuing a surprise of ink on paper
Secrets of the demure flesh
The mind catching the eye watching
The body revealing its vocabulary
Tit thigh head hair arms askew.

"The only Mohawk afraid of heights"
This missionary from Holstein, Ont.
Descends on us weekly in his perfect car
Leaving his perfect wife and hi-fi
Vision of fries smothered in gravy
Who has taught pianos the use of elbows

(and saxophones what a mitt can do)
and us palefaces, who ought to know better
that beyond Ritalin and the power of a Golden
the glossy fashionable already decrepit
the lecherous eye obsessed with flesh
through the electro-chemical nerves and fibres

To persist in a vision outside of reason
Where ink and mind caress the paper—
Accident the collaborator—
That girl dancing, spreading her thighs
Caught, redeemed, celebrated
A moment of breathing alive on paper.

Robert, master of the burping quip
With Jacobs cap and sausage fingers
Whose clothing leaped from black to blue
Middle-aged teenager, fan of stars
Saturday Night Hockey, Hollywood Squares,
We celebrate what you were.

reflects Owen's own increasing familiarity and comfort with the countryside.

Despite all the partying, work isn't neglected. Owen has Markle, Rayner and Coughtry discuss and explain their recent paintings, each time pointedly asking how many paintings were discarded to get to the few that were kept. Perhaps picking up on Richler's pronouncement that he writes with an awareness of his own mortality—or developing *The Ernie Game*'s critique of those who believe their childhood will never end—*Cowboy and Indian* feels especially suffused with intimations of mortality. Owen cites Markle's near-fatal motorcycle accident and almost includes the artist's beloved dog's brush with death. Rayner (perhaps ironically) shows us a painting detailing a suicide attempt.

Owen next embarked on a series of vignettes for CBC television, intended to be broadcast between programs. They were known by a variety of a titles, including *Faces of Ontario / Ontario Towns and Villages, Not Far from Home* and *The St. Lawrence … More than a River* (1974). The only example of these films still readily available is a later study called *Holstein* (1979), which was made for the NFB. An elegy for a small Ontario farming town (Markle's farm is situated nearby), the film captures scenes of the remaining few residents during winter. Most of them are seniors, though a few children do visit the local store. There's no industry left. The two largest businesses, the creamery and a handle factory, have closed their doors, and the train station has been shut down; even the last local blacksmith is about to pack it in.

Residents are selling their farms because they no longer have the energy or the strength to run them. Many of the people we meet are no longer even capable of caring for their homes without help. The elderly men sit around the local garage and bemoan both the lack of work and their inability to do any, while an extended sequence with the blacksmith shoeing a horse functions as a record of a fading craft/art form.

The area's history stretches back more than a century. In the first scene, a farmer recalls how his great-grandfather cleared the land himself in the 1800s. Many of the inhabitants are descendants of the original settlers, but the blacksmith now finds he doesn't even know his neighbours. In fact, the town is an anachronism. Several of the farmers pick up supplies in ancient horse-drawn wagons (one doesn't even have a seat for the driver), while sleighs share the local road with school buses.

One of the principal topics of conversation is the amount of travel the younger (i.e., middle-aged) people are doing. Some of them have gone to Florida to escape the winter. In contrast, one older fellow recounts the places he's been: Pickering, Niagara Falls, Huntsville and even as far away as Bancroft, a couple of hundred miles away. (He doesn't feel the need to revisit them, or to leave town at all now.) This need to travel seems especially strange to the few remaining inhabitants since they remember when you couldn't leave the farm because it was absolutely essential to work every day. The fact that the world has gotten smaller has only made Holstein more remote and isolated. The old Protestant pioneer mentality is doomed.

Holstein recalls the outsiders' stereotypes of Canada as a vast, empty country covered in snow mentioned at the beginning of *Cowboy and Indian*. The emphasis is very different, as the entire film illustrates the death of a lifestyle. *Holstein* is reminiscent of the fifties film *Les raquetteurs* in its portrayal of a specific community, but the earlier film is full of vitality and at least partially celebratory; *Holstein* is utterly elegiac. A sequence with an older couple playing a jig by themselves is the liveliest in the film.

Owen next worked on *The Collaborators*, a detective series produced by the CBC from 1974 to 1976. The series is particularly interesting because of the way it was produced, relying on established filmmakers as opposed to TV directors. For example, Don Shebib, Allan King and Peter Carter (*The Rowdyman* [1972]) also contributed episodes. The segments were basically split into two sections, focusing initially on detectives as they investigate crimes and then forensic scientists as they unravel complexities or provide evidence. In several of the episodes, the writers outlined a Montreal-Toronto rivalry. Owen directed three episodes, all of which pick up on or introduce certain motifs in his work.

A Little Something for the Old Age (1974), written by Tony Sheer, concentrates on a cash-strapped former safecracker, Eddie (Sean McCann), who is forced to take one final job in order to pay for his daughter's education. (*The Ernie Game*'s Judith Gault plays Eddie's long-suffering wife, Alice.) Eddie is saddled with two unseasoned younger crooks. The youngest, Bobby, is dim-witted and impetuous. Philippe, the one who sets up the robbery, is ruthless and ambitious and considers this job as the way to secure a place in a prominent crime family. The job goes down badly when the manager of a nearby store shows up unexpectedly and the rash, trigger-happy Philippe kills him. (The doomed manager's wife is played by Gilda Radner.) The cops, led by veteran Jim Brewer (Michael Kane), are on the case immediately. Because of the nature of the break-in, Brewer suspects an experienced safecracker, and he immediately tracks Eddie down but accepts his claim of innocence. As the police get closer, the thieves turn on one another and Bobby winds up dead. Eventually, the cops arrive at Eddie's failing shop just as Philippe shows up to kill his last remaining accomplice. Brewer saves Eddie, but his life is effectively ruined.

The episode isn't quite free of television clichés. The principled old pro versus the reckless and imprudent rookie is, after all, a staple of cop shows. The filmmakers overturn clichés to some degree by underlining the cops' close relationships with both former convicts (for instance, the friendship between Eddie and Brewer) and informers. Brewer's partner, Kaminsky (Les Carlson), is genuinely concerned about his gay hairdresser informer, recalling the sympathy for sexual outcasts evident in *Notes* and *The Ernie Game*. Eddie's dilemma is also presented in terms that echo and invert the oppositions in *Nobody Waved Good-bye*. Eddie tells Brewer, "Five more years and I get a return on my investment," referring to his daughter's ability to earn significant money once she leaves medical school. Of course, this is in part a comic boast, but Eddie also has to pay for his daughter's education. Instead of serving as a means of rebellion, here crime is effectively forced on the protagonist through economics, recalling the displaced Mohawks in *High Steel* and prefiguring Owen's final film, *Turnabout*, with its focus on class differences. This particular program raises the Montreal-Toronto rivalry in two ways: the crime family is Montreal-based, playing on commonly held assumptions that Montreal was a rather corrupt city; and the hairdresser stoolie mocking conservative Toronto and praising Montreal.

The Collaborators changed gears when Michael Kane left the program in 1975. He was replaced by the veteran Québécois actor Daniel Pilon (from Gilles Carle's feature *La vraie nature de Bernadette*), who saw his character, Tremblay, as much more of a regular guy, completely capable of making mistakes.[2]

In *Undercover* (1974), written by Lyal D. Brown, Tremblay goes undercover to solve a grisly murder in the Toronto Harbour. A radical American group known as the Cobras is presumed responsible. He's introduced to the group by Caroline (the Toronto stage actress Brenda Donohue), who's not the waitress she appears to be: Caroline is the daughter of a very wealthy American businessman. She was supposedly kidnapped by the Cobras, mirroring the Symbionese Liberation Army's abduction of the heiress Patty Hearst in the mid-seventies. Caroline, however, appears to be free to come and go as she pleases, and is heavily involved in the group's strategy sessions. Unlike her compatriots, though, she's not a killer and she intercedes when they uncover Tremblay's true identity and try to kill him. The show climaxes with a chase scene in the harbour.

The Canadian police are hampered in their efforts to solve the crime by Lundy, an obnoxious CIA agent, who turns out to be corrupt. Kaminsky, Tremblay and the others loathe him and constantly slag him and his organization—putting a nationalist spin on a rather familiar cop show device. The show also features a bizarre, Fellini-esque visual joke. When the Cobras rob the ferry box office, the guard on duty is extremely short, and they get him out of the way by stuffing him in a drawer.

The episode introduces several new concerns into Owen's work. During the investigation, the cops question the manager of the yacht club, who replies, "This is a yacht club. People who sail are not the kind of people who get into trouble with the police." The statement is of course ironic as heiress Caroline is already in trouble with the police. Interest in wealth, privilege and assumed innocence re-emerges in Owen's next feature, *Partners*, which he was writing at the time of the shoot. The depiction of Americans in the episode also foreshadows *Partners*. Even the American law enforcement types are sketchy, while the radicals are self-serving or deluded. During the final chase sequence, Lundy tries to kill Tremblay by chasing him in a helicopter, invoking American military disasters. One of the radicals is, of course, a Vietnam veteran. Poor little rich girl Caroline seems like an early draft of Heather Grey, the heroine of *Partners*. The focus on radical groups (and Owen's suspicion of them) would also resurface in *Unfinished Business*. The Montreal-Toronto rivalry is once again commented on: Tremblay gets Caroline's attention by starting a fight in the sleazy waterfront bar she's working in by picking a fight over the inadequate size of English-Canadian pint glasses.

Owen's most intriguing contribution to the series, though, is *Dreams and Things*, which deals rather presciently with repressed memory, mental illness and childhood abuse—long before these were daily fodder on talk shows. The episode focuses on a troubled, suicidal young woman named Bev (Carole Lazare). As the story begins, her roommate, Beth, is screaming at her to get out of the bathroom. After slicing her wrists, Bev opens the door and asks Beth if she's happy now. It turns out Bev is pregnant. While in the hospital, she's visited by Tremblay, who has served as her guardian angel ever since he investigated her mother's disappearance almost a decade before. (In the interim, he helped her with a prostitution charge.)

It soon becomes clear that Bev remains traumatized by her mother's sudden disappearance. She feels that she's responsible largely because her father told her that her mother left because of Bev and her brother, Rick (Frank Moore, from *Changes*). It's clear that Bev is utterly terrified of her father, whom she hasn't seen in years. Conversely, Rick has effectively put the event behind him, getting a job and becoming engaged. Bev gives her child up for adoption (despite the father's offer to take care of it and her), but her behaviour grows increasingly erratic. She flips when Rick won't introduce his fiancée immediately, accusing him of being ashamed of her because of her lifestyle. Throughout the film, in fact, Owen emphasizes Bev's lower-class manners and speech—not surprising, given her alcoholic father's brutal conduct, their poverty or the hovel they grew up in. It's barely a shack.

Convinced that there's more to Bev's mother's disappearance than he realized, Tremblay returns to their house and digs up the floor, discovering bloodstains everywhere. Kaminsky and Quinn trick Bev's father into thinking they know more about the murder and persuade him to confess. After she sees the evidence and hears her father's confession, Bev's repressed memories come flooding back, and she realizes that she heard her father murder her mother.

Dreams represents the darkest view of repressive authority in Owen's cinema and Bev its saddest victim. Bev is so terrified of her father—and of resisting him—that she denies her own experiences. Instead of striking back at her tormenter, she lashes out at herself, assuming responsibility for her mother's fate. One of Margaret Atwood's key premises in *Survival*— besides Canadians' fear of challenging authority—is that because this faith in authority is so intense, victims cannot identify the real source of their victimization.[3] Bev is a more tormented, more conflicted version of Peter Mark, or perhaps a mature Joey. At the time we first meet her, she's becoming incapable of repressing knowledge of the incident between her parents or of dealing with it.

Owen's presentation here of mental illness and distress is fundamentally different from that in either *Notes for a Film About Donna & Gail* or *The Ernie Game*. Mental illness is the primary focus this time, instead of serving as a starting point for another discussion (as in *Notes*) or as a partial metaphor (*The Ernie Game*). The difference is reflected in the fact that for the first time, we actually get to the root of the character's problems.

Like Owen's other episodes in this series, *Dreams* introduces themes he'll explore in later works, most notably an interest in class and the effects of poverty, though the latter is largely developed in psychological terms. (The effects of poverty would come to the fore most notably in his final feature-length work, *Turnabout*.) The poverty Bev and her brother endure as children has almost as visceral an impact on her as her fear of her abusive father. Bev is also set apart from almost everyone else in the film by her working-class speech patterns, which serve to make her nasty and vindictive outbursts more intense and underscore her outsider status. Like many of the characters in Owen's other work, she's incapable of accepting discipline. But unlike her predecessors, her rebellion doesn't serve any larger purpose whatsoever. Bev is a very uncomfortable reminder of our willingness to ignore issues like poverty and mental illness. The film's milieu contrasts markedly with that in Owen's next project, *Partners*, with its tony upper-class setting.

6

Across the Great Divide

It took years for Owen to raise funding for his next feature, *Partners* (1976). Originally called *Rosedale Lady*, it was co-written by Owen and Norman Snider, a Toronto screenwriter who would later collaborate with David Cronenberg on the scenario for *Dead Ringers* (1988). The first draft was completed in 1972 by Snider and was based on his relationship with his ex-wife, who was born into a wealthy family in Rosedale (Toronto's most prominent enclave for the ultra-rich). Owen and Snider reworked it, and then Owen finished the final draft.

Part romance, part thriller, *Partners* is a history lesson, a meditation on what it means to be Canadian, a study of a social class and an analysis of the relationship between Canada and the United States. The title refers to a love affair, business relationships (both legitimate and criminal) and the fact that the two countries share the same continent. In the process, the film also riffs on several of Owen's familiar themes, including English Canada's Anglo heritage and the growing American influence in Canada.

Partners

Partners was made at a very curious time. The mid-seventies represented the high water mark for English-Canadian nationalism, especially in cultural terms. Influential literary surveys like Northrop Frye's *Bush Garden* and Margaret Atwood's *Survival* were first published in the early seventies. There were also political/cultural tracts like *Close the 49th Parallel* (1970) and Susan Crean's *Who's Afraid of Canadian Culture?* (1973), an analysis of the struggling cultural industries in Canada, as well as best-selling novels like Richard Rohmer's *Ultimatum* (1974), a fantasy/thriller that details an American invasion of Canada. (The utterly unlikely premise of Rohmer's book was that the Americans were running out of oil reserves, and they—or, rather, their Texan president—simply decided to invade Canada and secure more.)

Needless to say, many of these texts were driven by a fear/mistrust of Americans, echoing Hugh MacLennan's assessment of Confederation—that it was the result of the existing provinces' "mutual determination not to become American states."[1] *Partners* is the best cinematic example of this sensibility. The tagline for the ads and posters was "In 1812 the Americans tried to invade Canada. They're still trying." However, it is far from a simplistic condemnation of the United States; instead, the film explores the two competing cultural influences in English Canada and opposes cautious Anglo stasis and repression against energetic but destructive American greed and ambition.

The film's protagonists are the American Paul Howard (Michael Margotta), a drug dealer, thief and corporate spy, and the ultra-WASP heiress Heather Grey (Hollis McLaren). Grey's family were descendants of United Empire Loyalists, a group of Americans who remained loyal to the British Empire and came to Canada during and after the American Revolution in the late eighteenth century. Essentially, this influx of Anglos changed Canada from a predominantly French colony to an English outpost. The lingering effect of this within the Canadian polity in contemporary terms was that "Ontario was ... determined to insist upon its own image as the British fact in Canada."[2] Howard comes to Toronto to abet an American conglomerate's hostile takeover bid for the Canadian Pulp and Paper Company, founded by the progenitor of the Grey family, Sir Adam, now owned and operated by Heather's father, John Grey (Denholm Elliott).

In the opening, Owen cross-cuts between three events. Heather is at home analyzing a maple leaf under a microscope (a rather obvious symbol for what follows), cutting off a piece of it and then photographing it. Paul hops in a cab, passing a crowd of stuffed shirts, John Grey among them, as they enter a concert at Massey Hall. He breaks into the Grey household to photograph some documents, unaware that Heather is home. She discovers him just as her parents and their guests are returning from the symphony. Heather hides Paul in the back of the house, leaving him to stew for a rather long time, establishing the power dynamic. Eventually she's forced to introduce him to her father. Left alone, Paul and Heather flirt with/insult each other in a kind of sexually charged verbal joust. They even circle around a preposterously large globe separating them. The awkwardness suggests a corporate merger or a diplomatic mission more than anything erotic, and in fact their relationship will carry an enormous symbolic weight in the film.

Partners

As James Leach notes, Paul and Heather see each other as stereotypes.[3] Heather is clearly sexually interested in Paul because he's a bad boy/thief and decidedly not part of the upper crust she's used to. Later, she sarcastically expresses disappointment when she finds out that he can read. In turn, Paul calls her a "rich bitch." Paul is confused and rather annoyed by the tony accents of Grey and his friends, and jokes that they sound as if they're auditioning for parts in *Mary Poppins*. Heather explains that they don't have accents, they have breeding.

The next day, Paul's employers from the Argon Corporation arrive. One of them, Richard Hayes, looks like a conventional businessman; the other, Phil Rudd, has a very shady past and has been involved with skullduggery in South America, an allusion to clandestine American operations (corporate and government) in countries like Chile and

Argentina. John Grey reluctantly meets with Hayes but gives him the brush-off.

Heather and Paul meet again for a tryst at Paul's place—a beautiful apartment decorated hippie style, with a far more welcoming atmosphere than the Grey mansion. Paul is actually pretty well off, but unlike the Greys' his wealth isn't accompanied by social position. Another verbal joust ensues, this one focusing on how they'll describe what they're about to do. Heather decides to settle on "a mutual exchange of fantasies." These semi-combative encounters are primarily about power and expectations (recalling the fiscal language in *Nobody Waved Good-bye*). The blocking of the scene again separates them: when they finally decide to have sex they strip on opposite sides of the bed.

Partners

Paul enlists Heather to help him with a drug deal, and they head south of the border to meet his contact/supplier (Delroy Lindo). Heather displays her "breeding" and composure by responding to the dealer's comments about her lack of nerve by making an equally crass remark about race. Paul resolves the situation by insisting that the deal won't go down without "the help of my lady." Heather winds up playing an instrumental role, bringing the vaccination certificate for the dog whose cage the drugs are hidden in. A typical American, Paul forgets the papers, presumably because he considers the border insignificant. Again touting her upbringing, Heather tells Paul, "The thing about people like me is that we really are together."

Paul visits an old friend (played by the musician and composer Murray McLauchlan) in a recording studio and is surprised by Rudd. He tells Heather, still unaware of his actual purpose, that he needs to hide out, so she invites him to her family's "cottage," which turns out to be a massive mansion up north. The Greys have owned the land for centuries, and it was the source of their wealth. (The Anglo connection is underscored even by the car Heather drives: a huge contraption similar to Don Francks's Bentley in *Toronto Jazz*—with the steering wheel on the right.)

Her parents and her eccentric adventurer aunt Margo are there, drinking tea and eating cucumber-and-cheese sandwiches. Paul bonds with Grey—a strong-willed, do-it-yourself kind of guy—when he helps him repair his dock, wandering into the water despite the fact that he's wearing a rather spiffy three-piece suit. Hayes shows up unexpectedly (he's dropped off by helicopter) and makes another offer for the company.

Grey is livid, seeing Hayes's visit as a repugnant breach of protocol. He tricks Hayes into helping with the dock too, and the flunky gets drenched, which only strengthens the deepening friendship between Paul and Grey. When Hayes complains about his refusal to cooperate, Grey bellows, "I don't do business on the weekend. You arrive on my property unannounced and I haven't called the police yet. I call that cooperation." A soggy Hayes blurts, "Nationalism is a nineteenth-century solution to a twentieth-century problem."

Somewhat miffed that her sex toy is getting along so well with her father, Heather drags Paul up to the attic and they engage in a little role-playing, with Heather wearing an old military jacket circa 1812 and Paul donning a wedding dress. It's another negotiation, with Heather assuming the male role. When Paul gets too feisty, she tells him that "aggressive women make me impotent."

Paul discovers a diary written by Sir Adam Grey and becomes immersed in Canadian history, particularly the War of 1812. As the film has it, the war pitted former friends and countrymen against one another. In flashbacks, Paul sees himself as Sir Adam chasing an American soldier and former friend over the border. Paul tells Heather that he's amazed at how connected her family is to history and, like Ernie Turner before him, expresses his desire to become an insider, an urge that doesn't sit very well with Heather since it's his outsider status that makes him attractive to her.

Grey and Paul become closer on a walk around the property, with Grey expounding on his determination to keep his land (and by extension the country) as pure as possible. "It's a special privilege of this country, an untrammelled environment," he explains. Grey, who's motivated by noblesse oblige, clearly sees himself as a conservationist. He cites a refor-estation project he was involved with, against his father's wishes. Grey is a classic Edmund Burke–style conservative in his belief that nature is not boundless but requires protection, and that he in turn owes the land his best efforts to preserve it. (In some ways he's a Canadian version of Burt Lancaster's sympathetic, doomed aristocrat in *The Leopard* [1963], directed by Luchino Visconti.) He and Paul wander off to visit a tenant and old friend of Grey's, indicating that his sympathies and his instincts are not class-bound. On the way home, a drunken Grey refuses Paul's help as he tries to traverse a stream, and this time Grey winds up in the drink.

The next day, Grey calls some of his political contacts to suss out what's going on with Argon, particularly how they acquired so much inside knowledge about his company. He spots Paul out of the corner of his eye and suspects that he's spying on him. Heather and Paul head back to the city to unload the cocaine they smuggled earlier. At a nightclub, Rudd again confronts Paul and pushes him to move more quickly. Paul tells

Rudd that they might be able to use Heather, since she has proxies that could aid a takeover bid.

Meanwhile, Heather dances with Paul's lesbian friend Barbara (Judith  Gault). Owen and Snider hint at Heather's possible bisexuality several times in the film, through her relationship with Barbara and her penchant for stylish pantsuits and fedoras. (This ensemble is usually beige, befitting her background.) The band is Rough Trade, then an underground alternative group specializing in songs about the demimonde. Significantly, the song is "My Fault," a statement of liberation by accepting ownership of one's desires ("Throughout the ages I've been repressed / Till I learned to repress myself"). The buyer, an old friend of Paul's, warns him about Rudd's past and his apparently murderous activities in South America.

Paul decides to back out of the deal and aid the Greys instead. Grey's board of directors is keen on the new Argon bid, meaning Grey could lose control of the company. His closest friend tells him that his thinking is backwards, and he must decide if he wants to run a multinational

Partners

company or a machine shop in his garage. As all this is going on, Heather and Barbara take photographs of some houses due to be torn down, and they wind up getting arrested, echoing the moment of rupture/self-definition from *Nobody Waved Good-bye*. Tellingly, Heather commits a crime by trying to preserve something, much like her father. (Ironically, given her propertied status and her father's earlier threats against Hayes, the crime is trespassing.) Her act is even less appreciated than her father's efforts, as the locals call the cops, confusing her with one of the developers. Her brief period in jail awakens Heather to how protected she's been all her life. (Jackie Burroughs and Michèle Chicoine, the principals of *Notes for a Film About Donna & Gail*, have cameos in the jailhouse scene.)

Paul arranges a meeting with Grey and Gordon, the head of Argon, who's unaware of how badly things have been going. Grey and Gordon are both private-school old boys and get along famously. (One of Grey's major objections to the bid is that he's been approached only by errand boys, another breach of protocol for him.) At a going-away party for Heather's crazy aunt Margo, Grey and Gordon hash out a deal, but Grey is accidentally killed by an enraged Rudd, who was actually aiming at Paul. Significantly, this occurs at the same place as Paul's Adam Grey flashbacks/fantasies. Paul returns to the States, and Heather takes over her father's company, determined not to "sell out to the Americans."

Partners doesn't so much reverse *Nobody Waved Good-bye*'s assessment of Anglo and American influences as look at them from a different, more complicated perspective. As James Leach states, the film makes explicit what was partly implicit in *Nobody Waved Good-bye*.[4] The Greys very much belong to the old, repressive English-Scottish order, tracing their history back virtually to its Canadian origin. One of the reasons for the greater complexity is the Greys' wealth—indeed, the film struggles to correct the stereotypes Paul has about Heather and the upper classes in general and vice versa. Wealth gives the Greys certain advantages (certainly far more than the Marks), but it's not as if they're free of all constraints. Heather's dispute with Paul's drug supplier is partially based on his claim of invincibility, which he attributes to his growing wealth.

As Owen and Snider have it, it's the women from this class who suffer the most from its repressive, rigid heritage. (As we've seen, Owen's interest in feminism stretches back to *Notes*.) Eccentric Aunt Margo, whom Heather idolizes, was ostracized for her unconventional decisions, while her niece feels oppressed by the substantial amount of history behind her. She specifically describes it as a weight on her back that she's carried since childhood. Following her arrest, she tells Paul and her father, "I feel like I've been living in a closet all my life." Heather is rich and very well cared for, but she has no real power of her own. Her father expects her to use her proxies as he tells her to.

John Grey has his own burdens to deal with. He discovers that neither money, national boundaries, social status nor even political clout (his friend in Parliament isn't able to help him) can protect him from everything. And certainly not multinational corporations. He's desperately trying to retain ownership of his own company, fighting off wealthier companies who could simply buy Canadian Pulp and Paper out from underneath him. Even his board is attracted by the bid, effectively abandoning him. The potential loss of the company stings even more because it threatens his heritage and legacy, symbolized in his concern for the countryside and his intimate relationship with his land. (Unlike his American counterparts, he's happy to get his hands dirty.)

Partners

At the same time, Grey's insistence on observing certain proprieties—part of his WASP background—is equated with stubbornness and outmoded thinking. Grey resents dealing with flunkies and foolhardily dismisses the initial offer peremptorily, failing to investigate it any further. (In a typically arrogant Canadian upper-class moment, he complains that he's "never known a Yank who wasn't in a hurry.") Ditto for the second offer, which he dismisses even more brusquely. His solution is to fall back on family ties, using Heather's proxies to stave off the takeover. When she fails to show up at the meeting because she's just been arrested, he's placed in an impossible position as his board is more interested in money than in saving the company. Even Grey's closest friend salivates at the American offer and tells him he needs to wake up and decide whether he wants to run a major international company or give it all up. Then there's his pig-headed refusal of Paul's help when they're crossing the river. His belief in property and boundaries is likewise called into question. As he finds out, he doesn't really own his company, since he has to placate his board. Ironically, even his own relatively dutiful daughter is eventually arrested for trespassing. As his death suggests, the old ways of doing things are doomed. In the end, it's Heather who has to take up the fight—but unlike her father she's not as easily swayed by old-boy courtesies.

Conversely, the Americans do business in a very different way. Throughout the film they are associated with subterfuge and underhandedness. The first emissary from Argon is Paul, a spy and a thief, and the first "overture" from Argon is a break-in. Propriety is completely dispensed with. There is no distinction between private life and business, never mind the weekend. Rudd urges Paul to press Heather for more information so he can use it in the takeover bid. Paul himself is not entirely opposed to this, at least in the beginning. Pushed by Rudd, Paul even puts Heather in jeopardy by telling him about her proxies. Contrast this with Adam Grey's refusal in the fantasy sequence to shoot at his departing friend.

This portrait of Americans as immoral businessmen is strengthened and expanded to include the entire country's sensibility via Rudd's connection to covert actions and murder in South America—and is further buttressed by Hayes's arrival at the Grey cottage in the seventies symbol for American military misadventures and power: the helicopter. The violence and crassness of American multinational capitalism is similarly proven by the death of an innocent bystander, Grey. Even the moderately sympathetic Gordon is aware of these activities. He keeps telling Hayes and Rudd that this deal "is not a South American situation" and that they have to be careful not to offend the locals.

The Americans invariably condescend to their Canadian counterparts, treating them like quaint hicks. Hayes crassly describes Grey and others as being "as nervous as virgins at an orgy." (Like Edmund Wilson, they see Canada as a large, unpopulated store of natural resources, theirs for the taking.) Owen and Snider constantly emphasize the Americans' separation from the land, evident in the scene where Grey cons Paul and Hayes into helping them with his dock and gets both of them drenched. It's equally significant that Paul and Hayes are so inappropriately attired for a visit to the country, which confirms Grey's belief that they're simply overdressed classless hustlers, ignorant of decorum.

Yet it's equally true that English Canadians like Grey play into this stereotype. Grey rambles on and on about the purity of the countryside, as if Canada was just a huge wildlife preserve. Of course, it's *his* wildlife preserve, property he owns. The entire business with the dock plays like a joke about a yokel one-upping arrogant city slickers.

Like Ernie's businessman accomplice, Americans are seen here as catalysts. Paul inspires Heather's rebellion against her background, opening her eyes to sexual experimentation and providing her the opportunity to do more than play at photography. They're also seen as harbingers of an inevitable future. As John Grey's dilemma indicates, it's unwise to assume that national boundaries will necessarily preserve the status quo, and certainly not the "untrammelled wilderness" he adores.

At the same time, even as it outlines these differences, *Partners* complicates the notion of nationality, acknowledging the two countries' shared histories. In the flashbacks to the War of 1812, the two antagonists are indistinguishable from each other. Moreover, Heather persistently refutes the notion that Sir Adam Grey's efforts were somehow noble. She tells Paul that Adam Grey was a thief, just like him, protecting his land with an axe and a gun. Of course, the land was given to him because he left the United States, which could be perceived by some as treason. Paul is further linked to the Grey forefather when he carelessly fires his shotgun and kills a pheasant for no reason, which infuriates Heather. John Grey himself is part of this, though his version of gunplay is a social outing. At the get-together after the concert, he asks his cronies if they're planning to go duck shooting (as opposed to hunting) in Manitoba anytime soon. James Leach argues that this is intended as a critique of the capitalist status quo's aggressive phallocentric nature. And Heather, possibly bisexual and with an interest in art, represents a route away from the dead-end macho belief system.[5]

Partners

As in *The Ernie Game*, art, sex and crime are interlinked and seen as transgressive blows against the old repressive order. Heather asserts her independence by taking photographs and getting arrested. Paul, a thief and dealer, is the one who opens up these worlds for her. As in *Nobody Waved Good-bye*, the protagonists commit various criminal acts, each of which requires more agency than the last. At first, Heather only conceals Paul, an act that initiates her into his world. Then she twice assists him with the drug smuggling, which confirms her as part of it; finally, during the photo shoot with Barbara, she commits her own crime—albeit an entirely unimportant one—and is arrested for trespassing. Her arrest is a greater blow to the old order than she realizes, preventing her from aiding her father at the board meeting. For the first time in Owen's work, though, art serves a different, more immediate, social function; Heather's express purpose in taking the photographs is to protest against the destruction of a neighbourhood.

The developing relationship between Paul and Heather also suggests an escape from the status quo. As mentioned before, they initially regard each other as stereotypes: a rich bitch and a dangerous thief. Heather sees her sexual encounters with Paul as expressions of power. They are usually rigorously stage-managed or negotiated, like a corporate merger or a treaty. There's little sense of abandonment in her version of foreplay, which is essentially a verbal battle to see who's smarter and wittier. She is initially on top, as befits her class. The lyrically photographed love scenes, in which they alternate positions of "power," suggest a means of transcending the struggle that first defines their relationship.

In its early stages, their relationship is predicated on mutual use. Heather sees Paul as an escape from propriety and respectability (he is a thief, after all) as well as a sexual plaything—and he has the added benefit of potentially offending her father. Paul sees her as part of his assignment and, later, as an "in" to the world of privilege previously denied him. Things begin to change as they get closer and move beyond their prejudices.

By the film's conclusion, they have committed themselves loosely to an alliance. Paul says they have to find their own language and concocts the scheme that saves the Greys' company (though it's hard to believe that Gordon is as benevolent as he seems). However, their alliance is a long-distance one and somewhat shaky, as they agree to keep things open. Neither wants to give up anything for the other.

Paul is kind of an existential, counterculture rebel, reminiscent of the drug-dealing heroes of *Easy Rider* (1969), though marginally better dressed. But Paul is becoming increasingly disenchanted with his role, reflecting the disillusionment with drugs in the aftermath of the sixties. At the same time, he could represent the tenuous, modish nature of that rebellion. He's now determined to be part of the legitimate upper classes, as evinced by his speech to Heather when he tells her he wants to be an insider.

Like *Nobody Waved Good-bye*, *Notes for a Film About Donna & Gail* and *The Ernie Game*, *Partners* sparked controversy. The sex scenes and the

CINEMA
CANADA

PARTNERS

Partners

Partenaires... en amour, en affaires, dans la vie. Est-ce possible quand on appartient à deux mondes complètement opposés?

Heather, fille d'un gros industriel de Toronto surprend un soir un cambrioleur, Paul, en train de photographier des documents dans le bureau de son père. Ce cambrioleur, membre d'une bande qui pratique l'espionnage industriel, a l'avantage non seulement d'avoir de l'audace mais aussi d'être joli garçon. Aussi, Heather, séduite par une façon de vivre qu'elle ignore, se retrouve vite associée à sa vie et à ses aventures "professionnelles". Des aventures qui l'amènent à fréquenter d'étranges milieux, celui de la drogue, entre autres, où l'on peut être très "expéditif". Mais Heather et Paul découvrent que de jeu en jeu, on risque de se faire jouer soi-même et que les gangsters, comparés à certains hommes d'affaires, sont presque des enfants de choeur.

Et chacun continuera son chemin, chacun dans son milieu.

Couleur 35mm 95 minutes

Réalisation: Don Owen
Production: Chalmers Adams et Don Owen
Scénario: Norman Snider et Don Owen
Images: Marc Champion
Musique: composée et interprétée à l'écran par Murray McLaughlan
Montage: George Appleby
Son: James McCarthy

Interprétation:
Denholm Eliott (John Grey)
Hollis McLaren (Heather Grey)
Michael J. Margotta (Paul Howard)
Lee Broker (Philip Rudd)
Judith Gault (Barbara)
Robert Silverman (Hayes)
Irena Mayeska (tante Margot)

Don Owen / Filmographie

1962 / Départ sans adieux
1964 / Notes for a Film About Donna and Gail
1968 / Ernie

Société de production:
Clearwater Films Limited
436 Sackville Street
Toronto, Ontario M4X 1S9
(416. 920-0630)

Distribution au Canada:
Astral Films Limitée
175, boulevard Montpellier
Montréal, Québec H4N 2G5
(514. 748-6976)

Ventes à l'étranger:
Clearwater Films Limited
436 Sackville Street
Toronto, Ontario M4X 1S9
(416. 920-0630)

Produit avec le concours financier de la Société de développement de l'industrie cinématographique canadienne

Secrétariat d'État Secretary of State

Bureau des Festivals du Film
Ottawa, Canada

Imprimé au Canada

role-playing did not please Ontario's prudish censors, who demanded cuts.[6] After the film became a cause célèbre at the 1976 Festival of Festivals (now the Toronto International Film Festival), the filmmakers refused to make any. The censors seemed especially perturbed by the fact that Heather was on top during the love scenes—a telling indication that the old repressive order was still intact. Owen argued that the love scenes were based on classic Canadian paintings by his friend Graham Coughtry. Eventually, the film's distributor relented. When the film was finally released, the reviews were mixed, though it did have several defenders, including James Leach and the film historian and professor Peter Morris.

Like *Nobody Waved Good-bye* and *The Ernie Game*, *Partners* demonstrates Owen's innate ability to subvert the status quo. *Partners* was funded under the tax shelter law, a program officially known as the Capital Cost Allowance, which was instituted in 1975 with the aim of encouraging private investment in Canadian films. (It lasted until the mid-eighties.) Most of the films produced under this system were appalling knock-offs of American genre movies—even duplicating the short-lived vogue for disaster films—with Canadian cities filling in for American ones. Somehow Owen managed to use this program to fund a quasi-thriller about Canadian identity and history, a far cry from the usual fare.

Partners is one of Owen's best works, though its dramaturgy is frequently weak—attributable perhaps to his long hiatus between feature projects. The flashback/fantasies don't really work (Owen later commented that he had overloaded the content of the film). The relationship between Paul and Heather probably carries far too much symbolic weight to be believable. In general, there's so much stuffed into it that certain developments (for instance, Heather's burgeoning feminism) feel disingenuous. At certain times, the film plays a little like nationalist camp. Owen seems uncomfortable with the commercial straitjacket of the thriller.

These flaws are also what make the film worthwhile. The confusion within the film accurately reflects Canadians' attitude toward the United States, which is invariably a mix of entirely justifiable suspicion and complete paranoia. Moreover, the film's ambition and its willingness to explore these subjects in a relatively mainstream context make it unique in Canadian cinema.

7

Hand-me-down World

After *Holstein*, Owen made a television film called *Spread Your Wings: Tanya's Puppet Theatre* (1981), now lost. He finally returned to feature film-making in 1984 with *Unfinished Business*, an upbeat sequel to his best-known work, *Nobody Waved Good-bye*. A co-production by the NFB and the CBC, the film focuses on Peter and Julie's daughter, seventeen-year-old Izzy (Isabelle Mejias), who's easily as precocious as her father. Peter and Julie (both played by the actors from the original film, Peter Kastner and Julie Biggs) apparently married, but they're now divorced, and it seems to have been a rather acrimonious split, especially for Julie. She has custody, but the pressures of being a single mother and holding down a steady job (she's a disc jockey at a local middle-of-the-road radio station) are starting to wear on her. The relationship between Julie and Izzy has turned combative. In one of the opening sequences, Julie responds to Izzy's taunts by slapping her in the face.

Peter has probably fared worse. He's in advertising, and his primary responsibility is directing commercials. It's doubtful that any job would offend his younger self more; he's an entrenched part of the consumerist society, or as Izzy's boyfriend, Jesse (Peter Spence), puts it, he sells people things they don't need. Working in advertising is also one of the most prevalent symbols in fifties and sixties cinema for suggesting someone is corrupt or irrelevant or both, as in Billy Wilder's *The Apartment* (1962). (Kastner, incidentally, went to Hollywood shortly after *Nobody Waved Good-bye*. His first big role there was in Francis Ford Coppola's first feature, *You're a Big Boy Now* [1966]. Ironically, in subsequent roles he was usually cast as an advertising executive.) Both parents are failed quasi-artists, formed and influenced by their middle-class backgrounds, though ultimately we do see them battle their ingrained responses.

As Owen makes very clear in the opening credits, the Toronto of the early eighties is a radically different city from the one depicted in *Nobody Waved Good-bye*. For one thing, it's quite multicultural, a fact evident even in the music used over the credits, the Parachute Club's reggae-influenced "Rise Up!" It represents Owen's most positive view of Toronto, eclipsing that in *Changes, Cowboy and Indian* and *Partners*.

There are even actual places to go. Much of the action takes place on Queen Street West, a hub for artists and activists to this day. Owen makes particular use of the Rivoli, a hangout for bohemian types since it opened in the early eighties. Izzy gets a summer job bussing at the club, in part because Jesse also works there. (Jesse wants to be an inventor but makes a living from his technical expertise and occasionally working as a videographer.)

As the film begins, Izzy is preparing for exams and hanging out with her high school friends in the suburbs. The situation echoes the set-up in the first film, but where Peter Mark had only Julie, Izzy is influenced and nurtured by many people. We first spot her cycling home with her high school friends. She takes the first opportunity she can to head downtown to meet Jesse, who constantly demands more time with her. He's not above using her willingness to listen to her parents, especially her father, as leverage.

Unlike Izzy, Jesse does not come from a conventional middle-class background. His father, Carl (Chuck Shamata), is an ex-lawyer, but he gave it all up to become a painter/lithographer and eventually a social

worker. His fiery and far more radical girlfriend, Jackie (Jane Gibson), runs a homeless shelter and leads a group of anti-nuclear activists. After watching Terre Nash's NFB-produced *If You Love This Planet* (1982) at an activist meeting organized by Carl and Jackie, Izzy becomes increasingly politicized.

Izzy's involvement in this activist clique causes friction with her parents and her high school friends. Both Peter and Julie consider Jesse unsuitable. He took his socks off in Julie's living room, an act that deeply offended her, and Peter objects to him because he "wears a skirt." Izzy's suburban friends consider the whole thing weird and prefer to go shopping at the Eaton Centre (then one of the most splashy and newest malls in the country) than attend a protest with her, leading Izzy to dismiss them as bourgeois.

Unfinished Business

Izzy harangues her father when he shows up at the Rivoli when she's working because she's stuck with his generation's "dirty laundry."

Owen frequently raises the issue of a generational split. Izzy and Julie battle over music, arguing about the relative merits of the Beatles and the Clash. Izzy resents her father for not explaining the world to her and for not giving it to her in better shape. As in *Partners*, the film acknowledges the failure of the boomer generation to actually change the status quo. When Izzy accuses Peter of failing her and her generation, he has no answer for her. Peter and Julie have in fact become part of the middle class, going so far as to duplicate their parents' behaviour in the previous film. When Izzy runs away after an argument with her father, Julie calls the police, just as Peter's father did when the car disappeared. When Izzy is arrested following the anti-nuclear protest, Julie wants to leave her in prison overnight to teach her a lesson, just as Warren did to Peter. To his credit, Peter refuses because he knows from personal experience that this won't teach her anything.

Structurally, *Unfinished Business* is packed with echoes of the previous film. Like Peter, Izzy is rebellious and dismissive of her parents' values, gets arrested and runs away. Even the major dispute between Julie and Izzy centres on her exams. Just like the Marks, Peter and Julie simply cannot communicate with Izzy, at least initially. When her parents lay down the law, Izzy responds with increasingly outrageous behaviour, just like the young Peter. After getting arrested during the protest, she helps Jesse steal a van. This act only gets her in a bigger bind, though, when she realizes that some of her newfound friends aren't as virtuous as they claim. In fact, Jackie is planning to bomb the factory they picketed, in order to draw attention to their cause. (The major networks aren't interested in Jesse's videotape of the protest because they don't consider it newsworthy.)

However, these issues are almost invariably presented and resolved in different ways from *Nobody Waved Good-bye*. Peter refuses to leave Izzy in jail. Unlike Peter, she is not merely fighting for her right to make her own choices; she's concerned about other people's lives and feels guilty about her comfortable middle-class upbringing. She's far less isolated and apolitical than he was at her age. Most significantly, both she and Jesse elect to face their problems rather than run away like Peter. Izzy and Jesse call the police and warn them about the bomb, and instead of fleeing to Montreal as they originally intend, they decide to head home and face the music. Within the framework of this film, there is no "elsewhere," a notion Owen explicitly dispels when he has Carl, the wisest and most understanding of the parental figures, mock the notion of "the great perfect elsewhere," which he sees as an inherently adolescent idea. Moreover, despite the number of parallels, Peter and Julie are far more understanding than their own parents were. Peter even drives Izzy to the bus station to meet Jesse. He gives her a pep talk before saying goodbye, concluding with a warning that running away really won't solve anything. Indeed, Izzy's problem isn't too much supervision/repression but perhaps too little attention. She's neglected by both her parents at various points in the film. Neither Peter nor Julie can really have much influence on her behaviour because neither is ever at home.

As one might expect from Owen, art is seen as an escape route, but it's not valorized here as much as in previous works. In fact, Owen slams the pre-

Unfinished Business

tensions of artists during a scene when Izzy visits Jesse as he's helping a band produce a video. The spectacularly untalented singer pompously berates Izzy because she's from Scarborough (one of Toronto's largest suburbs). The bohemian community in *Unfinished Business* suggests a garrison like the jazz musicians of *Toronto Jazz,* but the characters here are far more belligerent and smug than Francks et al. Instead of liberating people, art becomes a means of falsely differentiating oneself from others and dismissing them. In addition, though the most interesting and sympathetic characters Izzy meets—including Jesse and Carl—are connected to art in some manner, they're not simply artists. Carl is a social worker; Jesse wants to be an inventor.

The anti-nuke activists are equally cut off, so motivated by group concerns that they fail to understand the ethics or the ramifications of their actions. (As he did in *Undercover, The Collaborators* episode from the seventies, Owen expresses his suspicion of radical politics and extremism.) While Jackie's politics are lauded, her decision to bomb the factory is dismissed on every level. Izzy uses politics to berate and one-up her father when he visits her at work, blaming him for Hiroshima. Later, after she's forced to spend the night in Jackie's homeless shelter, she tells her mother not to worry because it "was a good experience." She validates her encounter with the residents by seeing it, in very middle-class terms, as an opportunity for personal growth. (The scene also serves as a reminder that Izzy's problems are far less serious than many others'. While at the shelter, she encounters a disturbed woman who was forced into prostitution as a child.) Owen clearly sees this emphasis on group activity/group-think as problematic, though probably not as problematic as Peter's individualism. He under-lines the contradictions and ironies inherent in political action during the protest scene by hav-ing a wealthy woman step out of her limousine and pick up a placard, illustrating the trendy nature of activist politics.

Unfinished Business

Unfinished Business is also notable for Owen's revised view of the middle class sans WASP baggage. At first, Peter and Julie respond to Izzy's independence by clamping down on her, much the way Peter's parents did. As in *Nobody Waved Good-bye* and *The Ernie Game*, it's the female character who enforces social norms. Julie is the most upset by Izzy's rebel-liousness, going so far as to tell Peter to leave her in jail overnight. By the conclusion, however, both have tried to understand Izzy more completely and are less prone to throw the rule book at her.

Such a shift in sensibility is likely attributable to the sea change in Toronto itself, which is, as mentioned above, far less WASP than the city depicted in *Nobody Waved Good-bye*. It can be threatening—note, for instance, the scene where Izzy is harassed by a man at night while walking down Yonge Street and is forced to turn to Jackie for shelter. However, it's also far livelier and more welcoming. (The liveliness is a little overdone at times—there always seems to be a band playing in the back room at the Rivoli, no matter what time Izzy wanders in.)

Unfinished Business is not as accomplished or as influential as the original film, the performances are not as unique or thrilling and the dialogue seems stilted at times. That said, it is still one of his most exuberant and optimistic films.

Owen's most recent feature, *Turnabout* (1987), follows two fortysomething women from very different backgrounds. Upper-class WASP Alexandra (Judith MacDougall, nee Gault) is a bored, depressed lady who lunches; Crystal (Jane Gibson) is a working-class woman who seems to support herself either by working as a prostitute or living off government assistance. Both despise the lives they lead. Alexandra complains about her demanding husband, Allan, an art director (played by the painter Gordon Rayner, of *Cowboy and Indian*); Crystal is just as dissatisfied with her unemployed, alcoholic bouncer boyfriend, Sid (Reg Bovard). They both live around Cabbagetown, a neighbourhood in Toronto that is home to both the well off and the extremely poor. They haven't seen each other since high school, but they meet by chance in their local supermarket and strike up a conversation. Alexandra, who's looking for something new in her life, wants to meet again, but Crystal is embarrassed by her poverty and tries to avoid her. Alexandra eventually tracks her down, and they become friends. Alex is intrigued by the lively, alien nature of the housing project where Crystal resides and particularly the countless children who live there. (She lost a child at an early age.) Crystal is fascinated by Alex's privilege and embarks on an affair with Allan. They switch places but soon find themselves just as miserable as they were before.

Owen recalls that "I actually made *Turnabout* as an attempt to redeem *Notes for a Film About Donna & Gail*, in a sense, because I wanted to do something that didn't have a narrator. The girls are their own narrator. I really meant it to be one film—I thought of them as being one film: *Notes for a Film* and *Turnabout*. But there's even a relationship between that and *Cowboy and Indian*."

The opening credits for *Turnabout* identify it as "an improvisation" and the film has a decidedly casual mood. It's a relatively straightforward fable inspired by an Oscar Wilde aphorism that there are two things in life to fear: not getting what you want and getting what you want. The dialogue invokes the language of fairy tales. Crystal talks about "fleeing the palace" when she visits Alex's house for the first time. The opening sequence begins with "Once upon a time." Owen has the actresses almost chant the opening together, and in the conclusion they alternate lines.

The film is set up very much like *Notes for a Film About Donna & Gail*, shifting between documentary-style interviews with the two women and scripted action, even offering differing accounts of events—each, for instance, claims to be ignored by the other. On one level, these disjunctive accounts are less about knowledge than about their divergent backgrounds. When they both claim to be snubbed, the contradiction can be explained by their need to justify their actions and as fear and suspicion sparked by their economic situations. When they're living in Regent Park, they're each embarrassed by their poverty. When they're both rich, they assume the only reason that the other would talk to them would be to ask for money. It's in fact possible that both versions are true.

Neither woman is entirely trustworthy. We hear Alex lie about how happy she is with Sid just after she told us he moved out. We hear Crystal tell Alex how happy she is just after we've just heard her complain about how bored and put-upon she feels. The viewer's unease in trusting their interviews/confessions is emphasized by the fact that Alex and Crystal each tries to ingratiate herself with the viewer/interviewer at times. Their motives are, in fact, equally ambiguous. Alex is slumming when she visits Crystal's neighbourhood, getting off on the vitality but unable to deal with it when she moves in. "It's like the United Nations out here," she says to Crystal when she first visits, referring to the multiracial makeup of the housing project. Crystal simply wants to escape her hand-to-mouth existence. Both are actually quite naive about the circumstances they're about to enter. Owen also complicates the viewer's ability to read the different versions by having many key events take place off-screen. We never see Alex get evicted from the apartment in Regent Park or Crystal get her daughter back or Sid move out.

The two women initially seem radically different in attitude. Crystal insists on being in charge, or rather looking as if she's in charge. Increasingly taken with Alex's lifestyle, she does nothing to improve her lot except ask Alex to buy her more things, usually clothes. Alex assumes responsibility for very little until she hatches her scheme to switch places. (Crystal claims this is all her idea and that she manipulated Alex, though it's possible to read this as an idle boast on her part, claiming more responsibility for her actions than is warranted.) By the end they've each adopted the other's earlier anomie/disappointment: Alex is desperate to escape poverty; Crystal is listless and depressed. Class ultimately trumps the differences in their personalities. Owen supports this reading in the final sequence, when he cuts back and forth so quickly between the two women that they become indistinguishable.

Despite the class basis of the conflict, *Turnabout* seems less rooted in political realities than metaphysical ones. It focuses as much or more on the problematic nature of desire. (It's probably the film most influenced by Owen's Buddhism.) It is easily his most forlorn feature, perhaps because it's the only one where there are no escape routes. It's his only feature where there are no artists or even quasi-artists in significant roles.

As craft, the film is far from Owen's best. The improvisation isn't as charged or exhilarating as in his earlier work, though the performers are charming. The humour (never Owen's strong suit) is usually ineffectual, but the film does show Owen's need to play with form and push boundaries. More than twenty-five years after his first feature, he's still testing the medium to see what it can offer him.

Conclusion

A curious thing happened in the decade following the end of the tax shelter era in 1982. The group of filmmakers who had emerged in the sixties and early seventies were almost completely forgotten, especially in English Canada. There were laudable efforts to acknowledge the works and accomplishments of this generation (primarily through monographs published by the Canadian Film Institute), but they were few and far between.

The tax shelter regulations, which resulted in an undue, perverse emphasis on genre films featuring has-been American stars, stalled the careers of many veteran Canadian directors, most notably Owen, Don Shebib and even Allan King (at least in feature filmmaking). Their own personal projects were shelved, and they were forced to work either with inadequate, minuscule budgets or on films (or in genres) for which they were temperamentally unsuited. After the conclusion of the tax shelter period, the situation didn't improve. Funding was in many ways even more difficult to come by. For example, Owen's last feature, *Turnabout*, was financed almost entirely through arts council grants. This only com-

Don Owen on the set of *The Ernie Game*

pounded the difficulties presented by Owen's rather lengthy lay-offs preceding the production. The vagaries of distribution didn't help either; feature films by Shebib, Owen and King were not readily available, even on video. As a result, Owen's reputation was consigned to one film—*Nobody Waved Good-bye*. This resulted in a rather twisted view of him as a staunch realist, when in fact nothing could be further from the truth. Much of Owen's work defies a comfortable fit into a particular style of filmmaking.

In some ways, the neglect is understandable. There was an astonishing wealth of talent that emerged in this period, notably the Toronto New Wave (including filmmakers such as Atom Egoyan, Patricia Rozema, Deepa Mehta, Bruce McDonald, Clement Virgo and Don McKellar) and Jean-Claude Lauzon, André Forcier and Denys Arcand in Quebec. It would, of course, be wildly unfair to criticize the positive reception, even excitement, that these filmmakers generated. However, it's not as if these directors sprang Athena-like from the head of a restructured version of Telefilm or the arts councils.

Owen's work, as I hope this book demonstrates, was historically significant on several levels, establishing fundamental motifs that are still explored today. Owen was one of the first English-Canadian filmmakers to respond to, and incorporate, developments in European cinema, in *Notes for a Film About Donna & Gail* and, to a lesser extent, *The Ernie Game.* Similarly, his portrait of the city as an alienating and inhospitable place set the tone for much of what would follow, anticipating the early work of Egoyan, Rozema and Virgo, to name just a few. Owen was also the first director to explicitly address our relationship with the United States in *Nobody Waved Good-bye* and *Partners.* Strangely, it would be almost a decade after *Partners* before other English-Canadian filmmakers such as Sandy Wilson (*My American Cousin* [1985]), Bruce McDonald (*Highway 61* [1991]) and Don McKellar (co-writer *of Highway 61* and director of *Childstar*) would pick up on this theme.

Owen was also one of the first filmmakers to assail the established order in Canada, addressing its repressive nature in *Nobody Waved Good-bye* and *Partners,* but also rebelling against it through his frequent portraits/defences of artists, an obsession throughout his entire career.

His work may seem curiously divided to some unfamiliar with the period when it was made. The heroes and heroines of his fiction films are conflicted—determined to declare themselves individuals but eager to be included in their milieux. His documentary portraits of artists alternate between full-fledged romantic manifestos and almost puritanical defences of art as work, sometimes within the same film. This contradiction perhaps reflects the inevitable ironies involved when any filmmaker or artist critiques his or her culture from up close—and dares to do it first. It's proof of Owen's courage that he incorporated these tensions in his work—and an indication of his sincerity that his work is seldom, if ever, glib; his rebels are never unduly valorized, and even those who oppose them are seldom given short shrift.

Most significantly, what one sees in Owen's work is an artist maturing and developing his themes in the face of cultural apathy, if not resistance. Thankfully, this resistance is no longer as formidable as it once was, and his pioneering work is one of the main reasons why.

When I started to research this film, I was immediately confronted
by the stereotype of the young delinquent (black leather jacket, ducktail
haircut) and by the enormous body of literature and film that deals with
him and the problems he presents. It took a while to realize that rebellious
behaviour is common to all adolescents, regardless of the income bracket of
their parents, and that although poverty certainly intensifies the problem,
young people from higher income homes were becoming more and more a matter
of concern to the police and other relevant authorities.

This is the story of Peter Mark, a seventeen year old boy from a
middle class Toronto family. Peter is in his last year of high school.

For the past year Peter has experienced a growing confusion in his
life for, rejecting the materialistic values of his parents, he has as yet
been unable to discover a more meaningful view of life for himself.

Peter's school work has been deteriorating over the last few months,
as has his relationship with his parents. The only thing to sustain him
at this point is his relationship with his girl friend of the last year, Anna.
But as Anna only too unquestioningly accepts Peter's confused view of the
world, their relationship tends to intensify Peter's problems rather than to
help him.

What's happening to Peter is something that frequently occurs to
people in late adolescence when they come to question the values of their
parents and of their society. In a way it's relevant to Frye's notion that
one of the more important jobs of a university is to shake up their students'
view of the world. To many young people this seems to happen in the natural
course of their life and without benefit of the kind of guidance that a
university provides. They may be sustained by their relationship with their
parents, or by some other older and understanding person who plays an
important role in this critical time of their life. But as with many young
people, for Peter there is no one he knows who can reach him at this confusing stage in his life. What this film will attempt to show is how
serious this problem can become if not helped, and what help may possibly
come when it grows serious.

The first part of this film is, in fact, Peter's first interview with
the probation officer, intercut with scenes that establish his background
and showing the kind of rebellious behaviour, at this stage, which decides
the magistrate to place him on probation.

The second and last part of the film will show Peter's growing
relationship with the probation officer, and how this effects the other
aspects of his life which are leading him in a dangerous direction.

The film opens with Peter in close up answering questions that are
being asked by a voice from behind the camera, as in a candid style interview.
The voice is that of the probation officer, and as this is his first interview
with Peter the questions to start with are merely factual for the probation
records: What is your full name? How old are you? At this point, there
are maybe ten questions and answers, ending with:
    P.O. Is this the first time you've had a police charge laid against you?
    Peter: Yes.

Peter and Anna riding through the city on Peter's motorscooter. They're
young and in love and we should see this and feel the kind of intimate fun they
have. We also see various aspects of the city of Toronto through which they
pass: the waterfront overpass and exhibition grounds, the large modern office
and apartment buildings, the raw and corny small-time atmosphere of lower
Yonge Street, the expensive stores and sidewalk cafés, and finally, the posh,
pleasant, middle-class district where they live. The music with this is a
kind of rock 'n' roll folk song, lively and sentimental, in the manner of a
current hit tune. Titles over this.

Filmography

Compiled by Andrew McIntosh

À Saint-Henri le cinq septembre, 1961
27 min., 16 mm, b&w
Production: Fernand Dansereau (National
    Film Board of Canada)
Direction: Hubert Aquin
Photography: Arthur Lipsett, Bernard
    Devlin, Bernard Gosselin, Claude
    Fornier, Claude Jutra, Daniel Fournier,
    Don Owen, Georges Dufaux, Guy
    Borremans, Jean Roy, Michel Brault
Sound: Claude Pelletier, Leo O'Donnell,
    Marcel Carrière, Roger Lamoureux,
    Werner Nold
Commentary: Bill Davies
Editing: Jacques Godbout, Monique
    Fortier
Music: Eldon Rathburn

La lutte
a k a Wrestling, 1961
28 min., 16 mm, b&w
Production: Jacques Bobet (National Film
    Board of Canada)
Direction: Claude Fornier, Claude Jutra,
    Marcel Carrière, Michel Brault
Photography: Claude Fornier, Claude
    Jutra, Don Owen, Arthur Lipsett

Sound: Marcel Carrière
Editing: Claude Fornier, Michel Brault
Music: Kelsey Jones

Runner, 1962
11 min., 35 mm, b&w
Production: Tom Daly (National Film
    Board of Canada)
Direction: Don Owen
Screenplay: Don Owen
Photography: John Spotton, Guy
    Borremans
Sound: George Croll
Narrator: Don Francks (uncredited)
Commentary: W. H. Auden
Editing: Guy L. Côté, Don Owen
Music: Donald Douglas
Cast: Bruce Kidd

Toronto Jazz, 1963
27 min., 16 mm, b&w
Production: Roman Kroitor (National
    Film Board of Canada)
Direction: Don Owen
Photography: Guy Borremans
Sound: Roger Hart, Ron Alexander
Editing: Don Owen, Guy L. Côté

Music: The Lenny Breau Trio, The Don
  Thompson Quintet, The Alf Jones
  Quartet
Cast: Don Francks, Lenny Breau, Don
  Thompson, Alf Jones, Michael Snow,
  Ian Henstridge, Butch Watanabe, Stan
  Zadak, Archie Alleyne, Terry Forster,
  Larry Dubin

Nobody Waved Good-bye, 1964
80 min., 16 mm, b&w
Production: Roman Kroitor, Don Owen
  (National Film Board of Canada)
Direction: Don Owen
Screenplay: Don Owen
Photography: John Spotton
Sound: Roger Hart
Editing: Donald Ginsberg, John Spotton
Music: Eldon Rathburn
Cast: Peter Kastner, Julie Biggs, Claude
  Rae, Charmion King, John Vernon,
  Ron Taylor

High Steel, 1965
13 min., 35 mm, colour
Production: Julian Biggs (National Film
  Board of Canada)
Direction: Don Owen
Screenplay: Don Owen
Photography: John Spotton
Sound: Ron Alexander, Roger Lamoureux
Narration: Don Francks
Editing: Don Owen
Music: Bruce Mackay

Ladies and Gentlemen, Mr. Leonard
  Cohen, 1965
44 min., 16 mm, b&w
Production: John Kemeny (National Film
  Board of Canada)
Direction: Donald Brittain, Don Owen
Screenplay: Donald Brittain

Photography: Paul Leach, Roger Racine,
  Laval Fortier
Sound: Roger Hart, Barry Ferguson
Editing: Barrie Howells
Music: Donald Douglas
Cast: Leonard Cohen

You Don't Back Down, 1965
28 min., 16 mm, b&w
Production: Joseph Koenig (National Film
  Board of Canada)
Direction: Don Owen
Photography: Gilles Gascon
Sound: Marcel Carrière
Narrator: John Vernon (uncredited)
Commentary: Robin Spry
Editing: Michael McKennirey
Cast: Alex McMahon, Anne McMahon

Monique Leyrac in Concert, 1966
30 min., 16 mm, b&w
Production: Peter Kelly for *Telescope*
  (Canadian Broadcasting Corporation)
Direction: Don Owen
Cast: Monique Leyrac, Gilles Vigneault

Notes for a Film About Donna & Gail,
  1966
49 min., 16 mm, b&w
Production: Julian Biggs (National Film
  Board of Canada)
Direction: Don Owen
Screenplay: Gerald Taaffe, Don Owen
Photography: Jean-Claude Labrecque
Sound: André Hourlier, Roger Hart
Narrator: Patrick Watson (uncredited)
Editing: Barrie Howells
Music: Bruce MacKay
Cast: Michèle Chicoine, Jackie Burroughs,
  John Sullivan, Ray Bellow, Aino
  Pirskanen, Gino Marrocco, Evelyn
  Gordon, Derek May

Two Men of Montreal, 1966
58 min., 16 mm, b&w
Production: Donald Brittain, John Kemeny, Roman Kroitor, Tom Daly (National Film Board of Canada)
Direction: Don Owen, Donald Brittain, Suzanne Angel
Photography: Paul Leach, Roger Racine, Laval Fortier, John Spotton
Sound: Barry Ferguson, Roger Hart, Ron Alexander, Roger Lamoureux
Commentary: Donald Brittain, Stanley Jackson
Editing: Barrie Howells
Cast: Leonard Cohen, Émile Legault

A Further Glimpse of Joey, 1967
28 min., 16mm, b&w
Production: Ross McLean (National Film Board of Canada)
Direction: Don Owen
Screenplay: Tanya Ballantyne
Photography: Richard Leiterman
Sound: Russ Heise
Editing: Don Haig
Music: Harry Freedman
Cast: Shaun McNamara, Norma Renault, Sean Sullivan

The Ernie Game, 1967
88 min., 35 mm, colour
Production: Gordon Burwash (National Film Board of Canada, Canadian Broadcasting Corporation)
Direction: Don Owen
Screenplay: Don Owen, based on original stories by Bernard Cole Spencer
Photography: Jean-Claude Labrecque
Sound: Roger Hart
Editing: Roy Ayton
Music: The Kensington Market, Leonard Cohen

Cast: Alexis Kanner, Judith Gault, Jackie Burroughs, Derek May, Anna Cameron, Leonard Cohen, Louis Negin, Corinne Copnick, Roland d'Amour

Gallery: A View of Time, 1969
13 min., 35 mm, colour
Production: Don Owen (Don Owen Films), for the Albright-Knox Art Gallery, Buffalo, New York
Direction: Don Owen
Photography: Reginald Morris
Sound: Paul Coombs
Editing: Paige Woodward

Crimes of the Future, 1970
63 min., 35 mm, colour
Production: David Cronenberg (Emergent Films Ltd.)
Direction: David Cronenberg
Screenplay: David Cronenberg
Photography: David Cronenberg
Editing: David Cronenberg
Cast: Ronald Mlodzik, Jon Lidolt, Tania Zolty, Paul Mulholland, Jack Messinger, Iain Ewing, William Haslam, Ray Woodley, Stefan Czernecki, Rafe MacPherson, Willem Poolman, Don Owen, Udo Kasemets

Richler of St. Urbain Street, 1970
30 min., 16 mm, colour
Production: Sam Levene for *Telescope* (Canadian Broadcasting Corporation)
Direction: Don Owen
Photography: Mike Dodds
Editing: Arla Saare
Cast: Mordecai Richler

Snow in Venice, 1970
30 min., 16 mm, colour
Production: Sam Levene for *Telescope*
    (Canadian Broadcasting Corporation)
Direction: Don Owen
Photography: Mike Dodds
Sound: Ivan Sharrock
Editing: Don Owen
Cast: Michael Snow, Joyce Wieland,

Changes
a k a **Subway or Spain**, 1971
30 min., 16 mm, colour
Production: David Peddie for *To See*
    Ourselves (Canadian Broadcasting
    Corporation)
Direction: Don Owen
Screenplay: Anthony Lee Flanders
Music: David Phillips
Cast: Frank Moore, David Phillips, Sean
    Sullivan, Elaine Werner, Mervyn Blake,
    Zal Yanovsky, Kenneth Dight

Far from Home, 1971
Production: Don Owen
Direction: Don Owen
Photography: Don Owen
Editing: Don Owen

Graham Coughtry in Ibiza, 1971
    (never broadcast)
Production: Sam Levene for *Telescope*
    (Canadian Broadcasting Corporation)
Direction: Don Owen
Photography: Mike Dodds
Cast: Graham Coughtry

Cowboy and Indian, 1972
45 min., 16 mm, colour
Production: Tom Daly (National Film
    Board of Canada)
Direction: Don Owen
Photography: Douglas Kiefer
Sound: Jim Jones
Narration: Don Owen (uncredited)
Editing: Don Owen
Music: The Artists' Jazz Band (Gordon
    Rayner, Robert Markle, Nobby Kubota,
    Graham Coughtry, Jim Jones)
Cast: Gordon Rayner, Robert Markle

**Faces of Ontario / Ontario Towns and
    Villages** series, 1972–73
Production: Don Owen
Direction: Don Owen
Photography: Don Owen
Sound: Don Owen
Editing: Don Owen

Not Far from Home, 1973
Production: Don Owen
Direction: Don Owen
Photography: Don Owen
Sound: Don Owen
Editing: Don Owen

St. Lawrence … More than a River,
    1974
14 min., 16 mm, colour
Production: David MacKay Limited,
    Ontario Ministry of Tourism and
    Recreation
Direction: Don Owen

Partners, 1976
97 min., 35 mm, colour
Production: G. Chalmers Adams, Don
   Owen (Clearwater Films Ltd.)
Direction: Don Owen
Screenplay: Norman Snider, Don Owen
Photography: Marc Champion
Sound: James McCarthy, Omero
   Pataracchia
Editing: George Appleby
Music: Murray McLauchlan
Cast: Denholm Elliot, Hollis McLaren,
   Michael J. Margotta, Lee Broker,
   Robert Silverman, Irena Mayeska,
   Charles Foster, Delroy Lindo, Robert
   Warner, Judith Gault

Holstein, 1979
28 min., 16 mm, colour
Production: Don Hopkins, Judy LeGros
   (National Film Board of Canada)
Direction: Don Owen
Photography: Dennis Miller
Sound: Suzanne DePoe
Editing: William Carter, Don Owen

**Spread Your Wings: Tanya's Puppet
Theatre**, 1981
Direction: Don Owen

Unfinished Business, 1984
91 min., 16 mm, colour
Production: Annette Cohen, Don Owen
   (National Film Board of Canada)
Direction: Don Owen

Screenplay: Don Owen
Photography: Douglas Kiefer
Sound: Bryan Day
Editing: David Nicholson, Peter Dales
Music: Norman Orenstein, Patricia Cullen
Cast: Isabelle Mejias, Peter Spence, Leslie
   Toth, Julie Biggs, Jane Foster, Melleny
   Brown, Chuck Shamata, Peter Kastner,
   Ann-Marie MacDonald

Turnabout, 1987
70 min., 16 mm, colour
Production: Don Owen (Zebra Films)
Direction: Don Owen
Screenplay: Don Owen
Photography: John Hertzog, Douglas
   Koch
Sound: Christopher Leech
Editing: Michael Todd
Cast: Judith Gault, Jane Gibson

137

Episodic Series Television

The Collaborators
60 min. episodes, 16 mm, colour
   A Little Something for the Old Age (1974)
   Dreams and Things (1974)
   Undercover (1974)

Danger Bay
30 min. episodes, 16 mm, colour
   Episode 57 *Love Game* (1987)

Acknowledgements

Any book is more than the work of one person, and this one is no exception. First, I'd like to thank Piers Handling and Noah Cowan of the Toronto International Film Festival Group for giving me the go-ahead on the project. (Piers's comments on an early draft of the book were invaluable.) Shouts out as well to Nicholas Davies and my excellent editor, Andrew McIntosh, of our Publications Department. Also, my gratitude to Sylvia Frank, Hubert Toh, Eve Goldin, Rosanne Pavicic and the staff of the Film Reference Library, who helped with research and photographs. Thanks to my trusty researcher, Amanda Phillips, and to my copy editor, Alison Reid (a better collaborator I couldn't imagine). The book couldn't even have been considered without the assistance of the National Film Board, in particular Jacques Bensimon, Laurie Jones, Carol Faucher and James Roberts. The Canadian Broadcasting Corporation also aided me immeasurably, and I owe a debt to Victoria Goodfellow, Russ McMillen and Laurie Nemetz. Thanks also to Peter Harcourt and James Leach, who helped track down key articles on Owen and gave me great advice. Marc Glassman and John Norris helped identify some of the more obscure figures in Don's early work. Also thanks to our hard-working and incredibly speedy designers, Linda Gustafson and Peter Ross, who made the book look great. Thanks to Tammy Stone, who came to share my enthusiasm for Owen's work, and to my Canadian programming colleagues Liz Czach, Stacey Donen and Ben Murray, who also critiqued early drafts of the book. Whatever's correct or insightful in my discussion of *Gallery* is due to the assistance of Leslie Korrick (who identified the works) and Andréa Picard (who gave me a five-minute crash course in art history and told me what I couldn't, or probably shouldn't, say). Norman Snider provided valuable background on Don and his work.

Of course, my special thanks to Don Owen, who gave unsparingly of his time for this book—and created some of the most intriguing and seminal work in English-Canadian cinema.

Lastly, I'd like to dedicate this book to my mother, Beverly McMahon, who didn't object too much when I stayed up all hours of the night to watch obscure movies—and to my wife, Kerri Huffman, who puts up with the result.

Notes

Preface

1. Edmund Wilson, *O Canada: An American's Notes on Canadian Culture* (New York: Farrar, Strauss and Giroux, 1965), 36.
2. Joyce Nelson, *The Colonized Eye: Rethinking the Grierson Legend* (Toronto: Between the Lines, 1988), 72–73.
3. Peter Harcourt, "1964: The Beginning of a Beginning," *Self Portrait: Essays on the Canadian and Quebec Cinemas,* ed. Pierre Véronneau and Piers Handling (Ottawa: Canadian Film Institute, 1980), 64.
4. Unless otherwise noted, all interviews with Don Owen were conducted by the author.
5. Hugh MacLennan, *Barometer Rising* (Toronto: McClelland and Stewart, 1941), 218. MacLennan's hero, a First World War veteran, muses, "But if there were enough Canadians like himself, half-American and half-English, then the day was inevitable when the halves would join and his country would become the central arch which united the new order."
6. Wilson, *O Canada,* 39.
7. John Metcalf introduction, *The Bumper Book,* ed. John Metcalf, (Toronto: ECW Press, 1986), 1.
8. James Leach, "Don Owen's Obliterated Environments," *Dalhousie Review,* Summer 1980: 283.
9. Margaret Atwood, *Survival: A Thematic Guide to Canadian Literature* (Toronto: Anansi, 1972), 18.
10. Northrop Frye, *The Bush Garden: Essays on the Canadian Imagination* (Toronto: Anansi, 1971), 228.
11. Joan Fox, "The Facts of Life, Toronto Style," *Canadian Film Reader,* ed. Seth Feldman and Joyce Nelson (Toronto: Peter Martin and Associates, 1977), 156.

1. Mon Pays

1. Taylor was a staunch nationalist who used his publication, *Canadian Film Weekly*, to advocate for federal funding and regulations to support Canadian cinema. He also founded a short-lived studio in Kleinberg, northwest of Toronto. Other contemporary Taylor productions included *The Ivy league Killers* a k a *The Fast Ones* (1959), starring Don Francks as a wealthy college student who tries to frame the leader of a biker gang when he realizes his girlfriend is attracted to their leader. Taylor also worked on *Now That April's Here* (1958), an adaptation of several Morley Callaghan short stories produced by Norman Klenman and William Davidson. For an account of Taylor's career, see Paul Corupe, "Taking Off the Mask," *Take One*, December 2003–March 2004, or Caelum Vatnsdal, *They Came from Within* (Winnipeg: Arbeiter Ring Publishing, 2004).

2. Paul Corupe, "Taking Off the Mask," 21.

3. Atwood, *Survival*, 171.

4. Like many Canadian filmmakers, writers and artists before and after him, Furie left for Britain. He would subsequently make several interesting movies, including the sixties espionage film *The Ipcress File* (1965) and the Billie Holiday biopic *Lady Sings the Blues* (1972).

5. "Recently historians have recalled Grierson's rejection of ideas for a commercial film industry, even when it meant fudging NFB attendance figures to win his point." David Clandfield, *Canadian Film* (Toronto: Oxford University Press, 1987), 18; "John Grierson was a key architect in Canada's marginalization in the film world." Peter Morris, "Backwards to the Future: John Grierson's Film Policy for Canada," *Flashback: People and Institutions in Canadian Film History*, ed. Gene Walz (Montreal: Film Studies Association of Canada: 1986), 31. "While some would argue that the practice of documentary cemented Canada's reputation on the international scene, it is legitimate to ask what kind of reputation this was. Achievement in a minor area of film may be laudatory, but at what price did this achievement come?" George Melnyk, *One Hundred Years of Canadian Cinema* (Toronto: University of Toronto Press, 2004), 69. Joyce Nelson takes Grierson to task for his scuttling of the feature film industry throughout *The Colonized Eye*. Hers is the most damning assessment of his legacy.

6. Martin Knelman, *This Is Where We Came In* (Toronto: McClelland and Stewart, 1977), 13.

7. The emphasis on compilation films also had a negative impact on the training of future filmmakers. In the Board's early years, few of the filmmakers knew how to do anything except edit. According to Julian Roffman, "They were all wildly engaged in making films, but none of them knew which end of the camera took the picture." Nelson, *The Colonized Eye*, 62.

8. Peter Morris, "Canadian Cinema: The First Six Decades," *Self Portrait*, 1. Over the years, countless Canadian filmmakers have complained about the American dominance of

Canadian screen time. The actual percentage of Canadian films on Canadian screens usually hovers below 5 per cent, though that number is somewhat deceptive since the percentage of Québécois films playing in Quebec is far higher, sometimes as high as 10 or, recently, 20 per cent. The percentage of English-Canadian films on-screen is probably closer to 2 per cent.

9. Nelson, *The Colonized Eye*, 67. The classic example of the early work at the Film Board is probably *Churchill's Island* (1941), which won the Academy Award for best short documentary. The film deals with Britain's embattled position during the Second World War and lauds the efforts of the British people, especially the civilians, in their struggle to defend their country against aerial attacks and a naval blockade. A compilation film narrated by Lorne Greene, *Churchill's Island* urges support for Britain not only to keep Canadians enthusiastic about the war effort but to encourage the Americans to enter the fray. Canada is mentioned all of three times, usually as a supplier of much-needed natural resources.

10. Michel Euvrard and Pierre Véronneau, "Direct Cinema," *Self Portrait*, 80.

11. Peter Harcourt, "The Innocent Eye: An Aspect of the Work of the National Film Board," *Canadian Film Reader*, 72.

12. D. B. Jones, *The Best Butler in the Business: Tom Daly of the National Film Board of Canada* (Toronto: University of Toronto Press, 1996), 85.

13. David Clandfield, "From the Picturesque to the Familiar: Films of the French Unit at the NFB (1958–1964)," *Take Two: A Tribute to Film in Canada*, ed. Seth Feldman (Toronto: Irwin Publishing, 1984), 113.

14. William Weintraub, *City Unique*, (Toronto: McClelland and Stewart, 1996), 281.

15. Ibid, 303.

16. "Wrestling … offers excessive gestures, exploited to the limits of their meaning … in wrestling, a man who is down is exaggeratedly so, and completely fills the eyes of the spectators with the intolerable spectacle of his powerlessness." Roland Barthes, *Mythologies*, (New York: Hill and Wang, 1972), 16.

17. Canadians do tend to adore good losers. Speaking to the former Montreal mayor Camilien Houde, Hugh MacLennan asked him how he could possibly have finished his career more popular in Montreal's Anglo West End, when he began his career as fervently anti-English. "That's easily explained … The English like a good loser, and I was a very good loser." Hugh MacLennan, *Scotsman's Return and Other Essays* (Toronto: Macmillan, 1960), 52. Witness also the enduring adoration (and sold-out houses) for the habitually underperforming hockey franchise the Toronto Maple Leafs—and the treatment accorded Canada's junior men's hockey teams. When they lost the world championship in 2003, hundreds showed up at the airport to welcome them home. When they won a year later, almost no one showed up. This tendency in sixties and seventies Canadian cinema is discussed in Robert Fothergill's influential piece, "Coward, Bully or Clown," *Canadian Film Reader*. Fothergill argues that the men in Canadian cinema can be reduced to the three types mentioned in his title.

18. Natalie Edwards, "Who's Don Owen? What's He Done, and What's He Doing Now?" *Canadian Film Reader*, 162.

19. Frye, *The Bush Garden*, 226.

20. Ibid., 227–28.

21. Edwards, "Who's Don Owen?," 162–63.

2. Everbody Knows This Is Nowhere

1. Jones, *The Best Butler in the Business*, 101–102.

2. "[The director of production] Grant McLean was furious because he had signed for the extra footage to be shot and knew it was going to be a feature." Gary Evans, *In the National Interest: A Chronicle of the National Film Board of Canada from 1949 to 1989* (Toronto: University of Toronto Press 1991), 102.

3. Kent's fascinating though scruffy first feature, *The Bitter Ash,* shares many similarities with Owen's debut. Like *Nobody Waved Good-bye*, it follows several characters reluctant to accept the roles offered them by middle-class society. However, unlike Owen's Peter Mark, the principal characters in *Ash* belong, or want to belong, to a distinctly defined group—bohemian Vancouver. *Ash* is far more a portrait of a subculture than Owen's debut. The group includes the angry, hipster/factory worker Des, whose girlfriend is pregnant and wants them to wed despite his reservations about married life; Colin, a pretentious would-be writer who expects his wife, Lori, to support him as he vainly tries to become the next Edward Albee (he's especially proud of his opus "The Man Who Killed Horses with Green Tails: An Absurd Drama in Five Acts,"; he's also a rather uncommitted bohemian, demanding at one point that Lori press his scarf); and Lori, who gave up the middle-class lifestyle to marry Colin but is becoming tired of their hand-to-mouth existence. Like *Nobody Waved Good-bye, The Bitter Ash* focuses on the collapse of middle-class values but also exposes the characters' self-serving natures and hypocritical behaviour. Another important film from the period, Allan King's largely improvised fictional short *Running Away Backwards* (1964), looks at bohemians and quasi-bohemians escaping middle-class existence on the island of Ibiza.

4. Don Owen, *Nobody Waved Good-bye* (Toronto: Macmillan of Canada, 1966), 12–13.

5. Ibid., 72–73.

6. Peter Harcourt, "1964: The Beginning of a Beginning," *Self Portrait*, 67.

7. Nelson, *The Colonized Eye*, 47–49.

8. Harcourt, "1964," 68.

9. Ibid, 68.

10. Owen, *Nobody Waved Good-bye*, 14.

11. Fox, "The Facts of Life, Toronto Style," 157.

12. Owen, *Nobody Waved Good-bye*, 14.

13. Ibid., 81.

14. These filmmakers would obviously provide their own perspective on this motif according to their experiences and the period in which they worked. For example, Shebib's Maritimers are met with complete indifference and vague annoyance, perceived as a pair of half-wit yokels. Rozema would attack hypocrisy and pretension in *I've Heard the Mermaids Singing* (1987), locating her film in the suddenly burgeoning art scene of the mid-eighties; the young immigrant hero of Mehta's *Sam and Me* (1991) would be seen as a means to an end by the relatives who were supposed to be helping him, and promptly shuffled off to babysit an elderly man. In *Next of Kin* (1984), Egoyan would follow a young man with no real acquaintances as he tries to find some sort of group that will welcome him. The heroine of Bruce McDonald's *Roadkill* (1989) is ignored by almost everyone she meets, including her parents, until she leaves the city. Cronenberg elevates this to an abstract, near-spiritual condition, exposing a web of conspiracies in virtually every piece he's made. Whichever form this took, hostility and/or indifference are evident in each film.

15. John Spotton, "New Film Features Improvisation," *Canadian Cinematography*, May–June 1964: 6.

16. Harcourt, "1964," 70.

17. D. B. Jones recounts a rather funny parody of this method in his biography of Daly. The satirical skit was allegedly written by Donald Brittain, whom Owen would work with on *Ladies and Gentlemen, Mr. Leonard Cohen.* Jones, *The Best Butler in the Business,* 118–19.

18. Edwards, "Who's Don Owen?," 164.

19. Ibid, 164.

20. Germaine Warkentin, *Canadian Forum*, October 1964: 157.

21. Brendan Gill, *The New Yorker*, April 24, 1965.

22. Fox, "The Facts of Life, Toronto Style," 158.

23. Chris Rodley, ed. *Cronenberg on Cronenberg*, (London: Faber and Faber, 1992), 10.

24. Piers Handling, *The Films of Don Shebib* (Ottawa: Canadian Film Institute, 1978), 2.

25. Wayne Clarkson, Keynote Address to ACTRA Toronto Performers, June 28, 2005.

26. Edward Said, *The Edward Said Reader* (New York: Vintage Books, 2000), 298.

27. Robert Fulford, *Marshall Delaney at the Movies: The Contemporary World as Seen on Film* (Toronto: Peter Martin Associates in association with *Take One* magazine, 1974), 36.

28. MacLennan, *Scotsman's Return and Other Essays,* 2.

29. Nelson, *The Colonized Eye*, 47–49.

3. The Lost Canadian

1. James Leach, "Don Owen's Obliterated Environments," *Dalhousie Review*, Summer 1980: 278.

2. Ibid., 279.

3. In his biography of Brittain, Nolan states that the other subjects were eliminated because they were too boring (Birney) or outlandish (Layton). Brittain recounts the

same story about Cohen moving into a fleabag hotel during the shoot; in another interview, Cohen argues that the hotel was, in fact, quite high quality. Nolan also claims that Brittain had to salvage the film. Brian Nolan, *Donald Brittain—Man of Film* (Amherstview: DigiWire, 2004), 130.

4. Woodcock quotes an interview with Cohen: "I never wanted to be in the world of letters. I wanted to be in the marketplace on a different level. I suppose I always wanted to be a songwriter." George Woodcock, *Odysseus Returning* (Toronto: McClelland and Stewart, 1970), 94.

5. Leach, "Don Owen's Obliterated Environments," 283.

6. Women in particular suffered when Duplessis was in power. Even in the early fifties they were prohibited from entering into contracts; from buying or selling goods without the permission of their husbands; from negotiating loans with banks; from having anything but emergency surgery without their husbands' permission. Until 1954, they could only sue for separation on the basis of infidelity, and then only if the husband kept his mistress in the house. Weintraub, *City Unique*, 279–80.

7. "I was about to shoot *The Ernie Game* … desperate to get going on it, and the Film Board said to me, before you shoot *The Ernie Game* you have to shoot this film … [It was] partly to make me get more experience working with actors." Edwards, "Who is Don Owen?", 170.

4. Undun

1. The key articles in the debate over realism as a viable course for a Canadian cinema struggling to find and define itself are included in Douglas Fetherling, ed., *Documents in Canadian Cinema* (Peterborough: Broadview Press, 1988). A Canadian variation on Pauline Kael and Andrew Sarris's battle over the auteur theory, the discussion originally involved Peter Harcourt and the filmmaker and author Bruce Elder, but eventually Piers Handling, Geoff Pevere, Michael Dorland and Bart Testa waded into the fray.

2. *Notes for a Film About Donna & Gail* is probably closer in theme to Godard's *Masculin-Feminin* (1965), which deals with contemporary relations between men and women.

3. Owen's film was not the first Canadian movie to deal with homosexuality. Jutra's *À tout prendre* touched on the subject, while Secter's charming *Winter Kept Us Warm* documents the increasingly close relationship between two young male students living at the University of Toronto's Sir Daniel Wilson Residence.

4. This was Burroughs's first film appearance. She would go on to become one of Canada's most prominent actresses, and is best known for her work in Phillip Borsos's *The Grey Fox* (1982) as well as countless television appearances. Owen first saw her in a college production at the University of Toronto.

5. Leach, "Don Owen's Obliterated Environments," 282.

6. Owen recalls: "We recorded another version of the film with Stanley Jackson, and

after a while I didn't like it. So I asked them to let me re-do it. He sound like an old-ish voyeur, whereas Patrick Watson could sound more bland … Stanley Jackson was a very prominent narrator at the Film Board; that's what he did mainly. He had been a teacher at Upper Canada College at one time, so he had that slightly prissy voice. I used Patrick Watson to downplay that aspect a little bit."

7. Edwards, "Who's Don Owen?," 168.
8. Leach, "Don Owen's Obliterated Environments," 283.
9. Edwards, "Who is Don Owen?," 169.
10. It seems especially odd when you know that the film was shot, according to Owen, during one of the coldest Montreal winters on record. He had to use two crews be-cause no one could stand the cold long enough to complete a scene.
11. Leach, "Don Owen's Obliterated Environments," 283.
12. Edwards, "Who's Don Owen?," 170
13. Ibid., 172.
14. Evans, *In the National Interest*, 122.

5. A Bunch of Lonesome Heroes   147

1. Edwards, "Who's Don Owen?," 174.
2. Mary Jane Miller, *Turn Up the Contrast: CBC Television Drama Since 1952* (Vancouver: University of British Columbia Press/ CBC Enterprises Co-Production, 1987), 32.
3. Atwood, *Survival*, 37.

6. Across the Great Divide

1. MacLennan, *Scotsman's Return*, 265.
2. Ibid., 264.
3. Leach, "Don Owen's Obliterated Environments," 286.
4. Ibid., 286.
5. Ibid.
6. Sid Adilman, "Director Defends Love Scene," *Toronto Star*, October 21, 1976.

Selected Bibliography

Selected Articles on Don Owen

148

Edwards, Natalie. "Who's Don Owen? What's He Done, and What's He Doing Now?" In Canadian Film Reader, edited by Seth Feldman and Joyce Nelson. Toronto: Peter Martin and Associates, 1977.

Fox, Joan. "The Facts of Life, Toronto Style." In *Canadian Film Reader*, edited by Seth Feldman and Joyce Nelson. Toronto: Peter Martin and Associates, 1977.

Gill, Brendan. "Current Cinema." In *The New Yorker*, April 24, 1965: 163–64.

Harcourt, Peter. "1964: The Beginning of a Beginning." In *Self Portrait: Essays on the Canadian and Quebec Cinemas*, edited by Piers Handling and Pierre Véronneau. Ottawa: Canadian Film Institute, 1980.

Leach, James. "Don Owen's Obliterated Environments." In *Dalhousie Review*, Summer 1980: 277–89.

Spotton, John. "New Film Features Improvisation." In *Canadian Cinematography*, May–June 1964: 6–7, 16.

Warkentin, Germaine. In *Canadian Forum*, October 1964: 157–59.

Selected Interviews with Don Owen

"Don Owen: Nobody Waved Goodbye." In *Objectif,* November–December 1966: 31–35.

Selected Articles and Books by Don Owen

"Adrift in a Sea of Mud," *Take One* 1 no. 6 (1967): 4–6.

Nobody Waved Good-bye. Toronto: Macmillan of Canada, 1966.

"To Oz and Back." In *Cinema Canada*, September 1977: 18–20.

Selected Articles on Canadian Film

Clandfield, David. "From the Picturesque to the Familiar: Films of the French Unit at the NFB (1958–1964)." In *Take Two: A Tribute to Film in Canada*, edited by Seth Feldman. Toronto: Irwin Publishing, 1984.

Clarkson, Wayne. Keynote Address to ACTRA Toronto Performers, June 28, 2005.

Corupe, Paul. "Taking Off the Mask." In *Take One*, December 2003–March 2004:

Euvrard, Michel, and Pierre Véronneau, "Direct Cinema." In *Self-Portrait: Essays on the Canadian and Quebec Cinemas*, edited by Piers Handling and Pierre Véronneau. Ottawa: Canadian Film Institute, 1980.

Fothergill, Robert. "Coward, Bully or Clown: The Dream Life of a Younger Brother." In *Canadian Film Reader*, edited by Seth Feldman and Joyce Nelson. Toronto: Peter Martin and Associates, 1977.

Harcourt, Peter. "The Innocent Eye: An Aspect of the Work of the National Film Board." In *Canadian Film Reader*, edited by Seth Feldman and Joyce Nelson. Toronto: Peter Martin and Associates, 1977.

Morris, Peter. "Backwards to the Future: John Grierson's Film Policy for Canada." In *Flashback: People and Institutions in Canadian Film History*, edited by Gene Walz. Montreal: Film Studies Association of Canada, 1986.

———. "Canadian Cinema: The First Six Decades." In *Self Portrait: Essays on the Canadian and Quebec Cinemas*, edited by Piers Handling and Pierre Véronneau. Ottawa: Canadian Film Institute, 1980.

Selected Books on Canadian Film

Clandfield, David. *Canadian Film.* Toronto: Oxford University Press, 1987.

Cronenberg on Cronenberg. Edited by Chris Rodley. London: Faber and Faber, 1992.

Evans, Gary. *In the National Interest: A Chronicle of the National Film Board of Canada from 1949 to 1989*. Toronto: University of Toronto Press, 1991.

Feldman, Seth, ed. *Take Two: A Tribute to Film in Canada.* Toronto: Irwin Publishing, 1984.

Feldman, Seth, and Joyce Nelson, ed. *Canadian Film Reader.* Toronto: Peter Martin and Associates, 1977. 156–60.

Fulford, Robert. *Marshall Delaney at the Movies: The Contemporary World as Seen on Film.* Toronto: Peter Martin Associates in association with *Take One* magazine, 1974.

Handling, Piers. *The Films of Don Shebib.* Ottawa: Canadian Film Institute, 1978.

Jones, D. B. *The Best Butler in the Business: Tom Daly of the National Film Board of Canada.* Toronto: University of Toronto Press, 1996.

Knelman, Martin. *This Is Where We Came In.* Toronto: McClelland and Stewart, 1977.

Melnyk, George. *One Hundred Years of Canadian Cinema.* Toronto: University of Toronto Press, 2004.

Miller, Mary Jane. *Turn Up the Contrast: CBC Television Drama Since 1952.* Vancouver: University of British Columbia Press/CBC Enterprises Co-Production, 1987.

Nelson, Joyce. *The Colonized Eye: Rethinking the Grierson Legend.* Toronto: Between the Lines, 1988.

Nolan, Brian. *Donald Brittain: Man of Film.* Amherstview, Ontario: DigiWire, 2004.

Vatnsdal, Caelum. *They Came from Within.* Winnipeg: Arbeiter Ring Publishing, 2004.

Don Owen, self-portrait, 1990

Selected Articles and Books on Canadian Culture

Atwood, Margaret. *Survival: A Thematic Guide to Canadian Literature.* Toronto: Anansi, 1972 .

Frye, Northrop. *The Bush Garden: Essays on the Canadian Imagination.* Toronto: Anansi, 1971.

MacLennan, Hugh. *Scotsman's Return and Other Essays.* Toronto: Macmillan, 1960.

Metcalf, John, ed. *The Bumper Book.* Toronto: ECW Press, 1986.

Weintraub, William. *City Unique.* Toronto: McClelland and Stewart, 1996.

Wilson, Edmund. *O Canada: An American's Notes on Canadian Culture.* New York: Farrar, Strauss and Giroux, 1965.

Woodcock, George. *Odysseus Returning.* Toronto: McClelland and Stewart, 1970.

Selected Books on Cultural Theory

Barthes, Roland. *Mythologies.* New York: Hill and Wang, 1972.

Said, Edward. *The Edward Said Reader.* New York: Vintage Books, 2000.

Text and Image Sources

All care has been taken to trace ownership of copyright material in this book. Omissions will be corrected in subsequent editions, provided notification is sent to the publisher.

Text

The poems *Ernie's Song* (p.55) and *Remarkleable* (p.95) were written by Don Owen. Copyright © Don Owen 2005.

The page from the original synopsis for *Nobody Waved Good-bye* was provided by Peter Kastner.

Images

Unless otherwise cited film stills and poster images are provided by The National Film Board of Canada and The Film Reference Library, © National Film Board of Canada.

Film stills from *Partners* are provided by The Film Reference Library, copyright © Clearwater Films.

Film stills from *Unfinished Business* are provided by The Film Reference Library, © Zebra Films.

The drawings of Don Owen (xii); Robert Markle (94); Don Owen (148); Don Owen (151) are by Don Owen, © Don Owen.

Film stills and posters from the following pages are supplied by Don Owen c/o The Film Reference Library: title page; 1 (2nd photo); vii; x; xiii; xvi; 71; 75; 78; 82; 106 (© Clearwater Films);130; 133; back cover.

The still from *The Mask* (p. 3) is provided by The Film Reference Library. Courtesy of Peter Roffman.

The following images were provided by The National Film Board of Canada © The National Film Board of Canada: 10, 11, 12, 13, 17, 18, 19, 51, 52, 90, 91.

The following images are part of the Cinema Canada Collection, The Film Reference Library: i (top left corner, lower right corner, centre insert); iv; v; vi; xvii; xxiv; 9; 14; 15;16; 38; 62; 63; 64; 66; 68; 69; 70; 80; 105; 107; 110; 112; .

The Film Reference Library is a division of The Toronto International Film Festival Group.

Steve Gravestock is Associate Director, Canadian Special Projects, at the Toronto International Film Festival Group. He has written extensively on Canadian and international cinema for many publications. Among these credits are the *Toronto Star*, POV *Magazine*, *Venue* and *Now* magazine. He is also a current contributor to *Cinemascope, Festival Magazine* and *Take One*. He also served as arts editor for *The Varsity*, the University of Toronto newspaper. His essay on the films of Bruce MacDonald, "Outlaw Insider," is included in *North of Everything: English-Canadian Cinema from 1980*, edited by William Beard and Jerry White.